"Jennifer, who do you think wrote those other parts of your diary?"

"I don't know."

"Did it ever occur to you that those other parts were written by other parts of yourself?"

"No. Not really."

"You've heard about multiple personalities, haven't you?"

"I'm not one of them!" There was a gush of desperation and anger in her voice.

"Are you sure?"

"I'm sure . . . !"

"Then how do you explain the notes? The diary? The voices in your head?"

"I don't know . . ."

"Do you *want* to know?"

She didn't answer. Turned her head away from me. Gazed out the window. She gazed with confused eyes, as though she wanted to form another personality at that moment, one that might fly to the tree, the wind, the sky. . . .

JENNIFER AND HER SELVES

Jennifer
AND
Her Selves

GERALD SCHOENEWOLF, PH.D.

A DELL BOOK

Published by
Dell Publishing
a division of
Bantam Doubleday Dell Publishing Group, Inc.
666 Fifth Avenue
New York, New York 10103

ISBN: 0-440-21287-1

Interior design by Jeremiah B. Lighter

Reprinted by arrangement with Donald I. Fine, Inc.

Printed in the United States of America

Published simultaneously in Canada

January 1993

10 9 8 7 6 5 4 3 2 1

RAD

To "Jennifer"

Contents

PART I
The Beginning
1

PART II
The Therapist's Journal
55

PART III
Jennifer's Diary
151

PART IV
Termination
195

Preface

S HE CAME to me as I had just begun to practice as a
therapist. She was a beautiful, talented young woman
who had that special awareness of other people's
thoughts and feelings—particularly the unconscious ones
—which is common to certain types of disturbed individuals. Never before had a patient induced such strong emotions in me—of love, anger, desire, and sympathy. I had
just graduated from a psychotherapy institute, where I had
learned the basics, but had not fully integrated them. Like
most novices, I tended to experiment more than I should
have, and because of the strong feelings the patient
aroused—feelings that reactivated unresolved issues from
my own past—I became overinvolved with her. This, of
course, is one of the chief hazards of being a psychothera-
pist, particularly in the beginning and declining years.

In a way, this case harkens back to the first case reported by a psychoanalyst—the case of Anna O.—described by Josef Breuer in 1895. Anna O. was very much
like the patient portrayed in this story, and her impact on
Breuer was very much like the impact this patient had on
me. Breuer became so obsessed with Anna O. that he
could scarcely concentrate on any of his other patients. He
visited her home twice a day, a practice unheard of at the
time, and spoke about her to his wife, colleagues, friends,
and anybody else who would listen. Most everybody
thought he was crazy, and his wife got so fed up with
hearing about Anna O. that, after eighteen months of it,
she had a tantrum. Breuer came to his senses and informed
Anna O. he had to terminate the treatment; but before he
could take leave of her she summoned him to her house
one more time, where he found her in the throes of an

hysterical pregnancy, twisting and trembling on her bed, rolling her eyes back, and muttering, "Now Dr. B.'s child is coming!" The next day he took his wife away on a second honeymoon.

Like Anna O., my patient was quite hysterical as well as narcissistic, and like Anna O. she used charm and dissociation to defend against the aggression that teemed within her and the constant fear of being annihilated by that inner aggression or the aggression of others. Like Breuer, I became obsessed with this patient, entranced by her, pulled as though by some mysterious magnetic force to feel and behave in a way I never had before. For a time, my life was centered primarily around her treatment. She began to recall and relive childhood traumas as though they were happening in the present and got stuck in this mode and needful of more and more of my attention—a phenomenon that Michael Balint, a Hungarian psychoanalyst, described in connection with Anna O. and dubbed, "malignant regression." She and I became intensely, symbiotically bound, caught up in a primitive dyad that led ultimately to a moment of truth for both of us.

This work is an attempt to portray not only a drama of madness and recovery, but also to illustrate the intricacies of a therapeutic relationship, with all its transference and countertransference, twists and turns, its joys, and its pitfalls. More than anything else, it is about a relationship between a very gifted but damaged young woman and a very human therapist.

ALTHOUGH THIS BOOK is based on an actual case history, it also represents a dramatized version of that case, one which preserves the basic truth of my case notes while allowing for a degree of licence in order to heighten the impact where appropriate and maintain the patient's anonymity. This licence is prominent in Part III, "Jennifer's Diary," in which I simulated a session-by-session journal as if written by Jennifer and her alter personalities. This "diary" is based on my insight into each of the personalities, their speaking and, in some cases writing styles, and my psychoanalytic projections of their thought processes. While it does make use of a literary device, the section nevertheless stays true to my notes on the case history.

I hope this candid portrait, with its occasional literary enhancements, will not only help readers to get a visceral as well as intellectual understanding of the two main players in this tale, but also a deeper understanding of themselves. In a real sense, we are all patients, and we are all therapists.

PART

I

THE BEGINNING

A TELEPHONE CALL

"ARE YOU the therapist?"

"Yes, I am."

"I was referred to you by the clinic. I was told you specialize in working with artists."

"That's right."

"I'm a dancer. Does that qualify me as an artist?"

"Of course."

"I didn't know if you just worked with visual artists or what."

"No, I work with artists of all types."

"I've been feeling . . . suicidal. I think I need to talk to somebody . . . right away. I'm sort of seeing somebody now, a psychiatrist, but he's not really helping me. I think I need something . . . different . . . more active. Do you think you'll be able to help me?"

"I don't know. I haven't met you yet."

"That's true. May I ask you a question? Would you say you're an active therapist?"

"What do you mean by 'active'?"

"Well, do you talk, for starters?"

"Yes, I talk."

"The psychiatrist I'm seeing now doesn't talk."

"He doesn't talk at all?"

"He just sits behind his desk and looks bored. And then he writes me another prescription."

"That doesn't sound too good."

"Is it asking too much, wanting somebody to talk?"

"I don't think so."

"Am I being overly demanding?"

"No, not really. Have you tried expressing your feelings of frustration to him?"

"Yes, but it never gets anywhere. He says I want to

control him. I don't think I'm trying to control him, but I don't know . . . Does it sound like I'm trying to control him?"

"I couldn't say. I'd have to have more information. When would you like to come in for a consultation? During the day or the evening?

"Daytime would be good."

"How's Tuesday at three?"

"That's fine. Oh, wait a minute. I think . . . yes, that's fine. I thought I had to go somewhere . . . it's fine, Tuesday at three is fine."

"Your name?"

"Jennifer Wells."

"Jennifer Wells? Of the Apple Dance Company?

"Yes. That is, I used to be. I haven't been with them in a couple of years."

"I'm sorry to hear that."

"I guess that's part of the problem. Are you a dance fan? You must be if you've heard of Apple."

"I saw you dance on TV once. On Channel 13."

"When they had their festival of modern dance?"

"That must have been it."

"You have a good memory."

"Thank you."

"You really do."

"I'll see you on Tuesday, Jennifer."

"Yes, you will."

SESSION

I

"I CAN feel this process starting again, and I'm afraid."

"Could you speak up a bit?"

"I said I can feel this process starting again."

"What process is that?"

"It's something that happens to me. It's happened before and now it's happening again." She was sitting on the edge of the leather chair, a tall, thin beauty in her late twenties with a downward gaze and a fragile voice and an aura that radiated vulnerability. Most everything about her looked vulnerable: the nervous blue eyes that peered intently from a pale face etched with a sprinkling of pink freckles; the dim eyebrows and lashes that were almost the same color as her skin; the long, wavy yellow orange hair, pulled ever so tightly into a ponytail; the faded, loose-fitting jeans, designed for a man's body, that hung lifelessly from her hips. "It always happens, this process . . . it happens right before I do something," she said, rocking slowly to and fro in her chair. "It's . . . very frightening." She was on the verge of tears.

"Do something?" I looked at her quizzically.

A glint of terror flashed from her pupils. "I'm afraid I might lose control. I'm afraid I might do something . . . stupid. . . ."

"Like what?"

"You know . . . commit suicide . . . or . . ."

"Or?"

"I don't know." She looked apologetic. "Or hurt myself somehow."

"How would you hurt yourself?"

She shook her head and closed her eyes. "I don't know."

I was sitting opposite her, trying to look wise, although I had never met anybody quite like her. I was in my early thirties and had just begun my practice. In those days I still had the innocent face of an adolescent and tried to compensate by wearing conservative ties. I was told that I gave off an appearance of naive earnestness—it came, in part, from my rural upbringing—but there were also lines of bitterness around my eyes that spoke of unhappy twists in that upbringing. One of my first female patients had once informed me before quitting that I was a boy trying to be a man. Patients, I had discovered, could keep you honest. "How would you hurt yourself?" I asked Jennifer again.

She opened her eyes, wincing. "What?"

"What are you feeling right now?"

"Scared. . . ."

"Of what?"

"Life. I'm scared of living."

"What scares you about living?"

"Waking up in the morning."

"You don't like to wake up?"

"No. I'd rather not."

"What happens when you wake up?"

"I have to talk. I have to walk. I have to think."

"And that's bad?"

"Yes . . . I don't like to think. I'm scared of my thoughts."

"How come?"

"I don't know. This . . . process . . . scares me."

I felt her fear. I could feel it from the moment she walked into the office, as well as other feelings I could not identify, among them a general overall heaviness, as though the very pull of gravity had increased several degrees upon her entrance. I also felt attracted to her odd beauty and touched by her fragility, but I checked the impulse to show sympathy, having learned that sympathy can sometimes drive a suicidal person to the brink.

For her part, she seemed from the outset to know I was feeling her feelings, and understood that she was having an impact on me. Her glances took everything in, and she saw by the way I looked at her that I found her interesting. She was a woman who needed to be interesting.

"Can you describe the process?" I asked in a neutral way.

"I . . . hear things." She fixed her blue eyes on me. "Voices."

"What do they say?"

"They're laughing at me."

"Do you recognize them?"

"My mother. It's my mother's voice. The psychiatrist I'm seeing says I'm just hallucinating, but I know it's really her. . . ." She rocked to and fro, hugging herself, gazing downward, her eyes glistening from the light of the lamp on the table beside her. "Sometimes my vision gets distorted. Everything in the room starts to get . . . funny. The room seems to decompose. Sometimes I blank out and don't remember what happened before. And then everything starts to feel scary and hopeless and I'm afraid I'll, you know . . ." She glanced up, frightened. "I guess you must think I'm a real nut case. I guess you're wondering what you're getting into."

"Are you afraid I won't accept you?"

"I don't know. I guess so."

"Have you ever attempted suicide? Or do you just think about it?"

"No, I don't just think about it." A sneer ran across her face. "I have a history of suicide attempts. I nearly died once."

"Did my last question upset you?"

"I'm not sure what upsets me anymore."

She hugged herself more tightly and gazed out the window at the courtyard that was bright in the sun. It was spring and the sun was cool and shiny in the courtyard, but my office was dark and her silhouette in the window was very still against the backdrop of the light green trees. Small birds were singing free of care from the trees to the left of the window as she sat in silence.

I waited for her to speak, aware that her hallucinating and dissociating was an indication of how enraged she was, and how severely that rage was jamming up her functions. I thought of asking her more about the hallucinations and suicidal urges, but decided that might be too upsetting for her. "You mentioned on the phone that you were dissatisfied with your psychiatrist," I said.

She was eager to talk about him and was glad to have the lead in. "I just don't think he cares about me," she said.

"What makes you say that?"

"He just sits there and nods. Once he even went to sleep during my session."

"Really?"

"Really. He had me lying on a couch, which I can't stand, and then one day I looked up and saw he had his eyes closed and his head had fallen back on his chair. He was asleep for about five minutes. When he woke up, I was silent, so he said, 'You're quiet today, Jennifer. How come?' I tried to tell him he had fallen asleep but he wouldn't admit it. He said he was just relaxing. I knew he was asleep, though. I hate that, when a therapist won't admit a mistake. After all, how can he expect me to tell him the truth if he won't be truthful to me?" She stopped and looked up. "Do you think I'm being too hard on him? Now I'm feeling guilty for talking about him behind his back. I don't want to talk about my psychiatrist." She was rocking again, and her eyes grew sad and wistful. She seemed afraid that I might side with my colleague. "I haven't had much luck with therapists."

"Luck?"

"They . . . I don't know . . . they always seem to reject me."

"Oh?" I felt a wave of sadness and yearning sweep through my body. I wanted to reassure her right off that I would never act like those other therapists. Then I began to wonder what she had done to those other therapists to cause them to reject her. "How do they reject you?" I asked noncommittally.

"Usually they get to a point where they say they can't handle me. The last one—the one I was seeing before this psychiatrist—he was a social worker—used to always get angry at me. He was the one I attempted suicide on. I took an overdose of sleeping pills and wound up in a hospital. He was so angry, he wasn't even going to visit me, then when he did it was to tell me he couldn't see me anymore. He said he had too much countertransference." She looked at me pointedly. "He made me feel like I'd taken the pills to hurt him, like I was some evil thing that he had to get away from. . . ."

"Can you tell me something about your family background?"

"My family background? I come from a family of dancers," she said, bored. Apparently, she had told her story to many therapists, and she did not relish repeating it again. "My grandmother was a dancer in Scotland. My father danced on the London stage. My mother was a Rockette at the Radio City Music Hall and a frustrated ballerina. Actually, both my mother and father danced at Radio City for a while, then she started having kids and he became a stage manager and she became an alcoholic. Now she runs a ballet school for children. I've been dancing since I was three." She looked at me and shrugged her shoulders. "Does that answer your question? Oh, yes. You'll be interested in knowing that I was . . . sexually abused."

"By your father?"

"No. My mother."

"How old were you?"

"I don't know. Young. I don't want to talk about it."

I felt slightly teased. She had offered the sexual confession and then had refused to elaborate. She had, I noted to myself, a sense of drama. I also understood she needed time to talk about such a painful happening. A silence set in and I took a moment to make an initial assessment of her.

I thought about the therapy dictum that a patient's very first communications set the tone of the entire treatment, and began to review in my mind her various opening statements. Her threat to commit suicide, I decided, was a plea to be taken notice of as well as a desperate attempt to compensate for feelings of absolute powerlessness. "Notice me," she was saying, "care about my anguish now, or else." Her contention that her previous therapists had rejected her and her present psychiatrist did not understand her was probably intended to convey the message, "Don't be bad, rejecting, and uncaring like my other therapists." At the same time, she was also warning me that no other therapist had been able to handle her. She was aware on some level of her pent-up rage and its potential for destructiveness, and she was offering this warning as a disclaimer, similar to the one on cigarette packages that reads "Cigarette smoking may be dangerous to your health." Then there was her remark about being sexually abused, tossed out in a rather coy way. This admission from a woman to a man, alone together in a room, had an unspoken aspect of seduction. "I may give you the privilege of hearing my sexual secrets, if you're good" was the underlying message. And she had followed this statement with a knowing look that said "I know what all you male therapists have on your minds."

I glanced at the clock, saw that time was about up, and began to consider the practicalities: how frequently to see her, how much to charge her. I had tentatively diagnosed her as a borderline personality on the edge of psychosis. I realized she needed a lot of attention to soothe her narcissistic wounds, and I was also aware that I was quite drawn to her and wanted to give her that attention; however, I did not realize to what extent I was attracted to her, nor how deeply I was already caught up in the challenge she presented me of proving my therapeutic prowess. I decided to insist she see me as often as possible. "We only have a few minutes," I told her after a while. "I'd recommend we start therapy this week, and I'd suggest three sessions a week for starters. How does that sound?"

"Three!" She glanced up in shock.

"Yes, three. Why?"

"Am I that bad off?"

"Well, you said you're suicidal, you're in a crisis."

"I know but . . ." She shook her head and looked forlornly out the window. "I don't know. I'm still seeing the psychiatrist; that would mean *four* times a week. I'd like to drop him, but I can't. He has to sign my forms— I'm on Social Security disability. You're not a psychiatrist, so you can't sign the forms. But even if you could, I don't know if I'm ready to let go of him. Maybe after I see how it goes with you. I don't know. What do you think?"

"How about twice a week?"

"That sounds more reasonable . . . but I don't know if I can afford it. As I said, I'm living on Social Security. I haven't danced for three years, or had any other kind of job since my first breakdown."

"Your first breakdown?"

"My first suicide attempt."

"How many have you had?"

"Two. Both times I was in St. Elizabeth's for a month. They diagnosed me as a manic-depressive."

My expression must have sunk a bit and I found myself feeling a little saddened by this new information, saddened that such a lovely, talented young woman had gone through these ordeals. There was a short pause during which she scrutinized me and I looked away from her intense gaze. "What do you think you could afford?" I asked.

"Not very much. I see the psychiatrist for free. It's covered by Social Security."

"The minimum rate for people referred to me by the clinic is fifteen dollars per session. Can you afford fifteen dollars?"

"I suppose so. Yes, I could handle that."

"Then it's settled." I started to rise.

"I have to ask you something." She held me with her eyes. "I want to know if . . . I can call you in an emergency. You know, if I feel suicidal. Would it be all right if I called you? That's very important to me, because I feel this process starting again."

"Yes, you can call me."

"And also . . ."

"Yes?"

"Also, I'd like to know whether or not you'll come to visit me in the hospital if I . . . attempt suicide."

I was taken aback. "Suppose I say yes. Do you think that would encourage you to attempt suicide, knowing I'd be there to visit you?"

"No, I don't think so. I think it would make me less likely to do it. The fact that you care enough to visit me would make me more secure."

"In that case, I'll visit you."

"Thanks."

"Shall we make an appointment for next week?"

"Yes, let's."

2

"WOULD IT be all right if I sat on the floor?"

"You don't like chairs?"

"Not really. I feel safer on the floor."

"All right."

She sat down in the corner by the window, hugging her legs, resting her chin on her knees. She did not appear quite as pale or desperate now. Her hair was loose, hanging down around her shoulders. A light shade of red lipstick lined her mouth. "I don't seem to have much to say today. What should I talk about?" She smiled squeamishly.

"Are you still feeling suicidal?"

"No." She quickly shook her head.

"That's good."

"I don't know what to talk about. What should I talk about? Do you have any suggestions?"

"Just say whatever comes into your head."

"Nothing's coming into my head."

"Nothing at all?"

"I suppose I should talk about my childhood."

"All right."

"Therapists are always trying to get you to talk about your childhood." She had a small pout on her face. "I don't want to talk about my childhood. That's all in the past. It has nothing to do with who I am now."

She sat in the corner looking up at me. I sat in a chair, my arms stretched out on the armrests, wondering what to say next, feeling awkward to be perched on a chair while she squatted on the floor below. I also felt annoyed that she had asked me what to talk about and then had said she would not talk about what she assumed I wanted her to talk about. I tried to hide these feelings of awkwardness and annoyance, but was not entirely successful. I am one of those expressive types whose feelings show on their face. In fact, I once excelled at comedy roles in my college theater club, where one of my patented expressions was the raising of my brows in mock consternation. "It's going to be hard to do therapy with you," I said, my brows rising slightly now, "if you won't talk about your childhood."

A nervous laugh bubbled out of her, then her face darkened. "I guess . . . I should talk about my childhood."

"That would be good."

"Where should I start?"

"Wherever you like."

"Should I talk about my mother?"

"If you like."

"I guess you want me to talk about the sexual abuse."

I could tell that she was feeling awkward about having opened herself up to me in the previous session, and I supposed she was also angry at me for being a therapist and for being male. She had noticed, she told me later, that all her previous therapists had paid special attention whenever she had mentioned the sexual abuse, and she viewed this fact, somewhat cynically, as evidence of male lechery. She also believed, deep down, that no matter how nice this man who now sat before her acted, he would turn out just like all the others.

I considered it for a moment. Actually, I *did* want her to talk about the sexual abuse, but not for the reason she projected onto me. "Do *you* think it would be of benefit to talk about the sexual abuse?"

"Yes, it would." She gazed ruefully down at the rug. "I'd like to talk about it . . . but it's difficult. Can you ask me questions?"

"When did it happen?"

"It started when I was . . . very young. I think I was about three."

"How long did it go on?"

"A long time. Until I was about eleven. It's hard to remember."

"How did she do it?"

"She used to make me . . . get into bed with her."

"During the day?"

"No, at night."

"Where was your father?"

"He was hardly ever there. He worked very late . . . he was the stage manager for the Radio City Music Hall. He never came home until three or four in the morning."

"What did she do? Did she come and wake you up and take you to her bed?"

"I'm not sure. I can't remember. Maybe I was scared and went to her bed."

"What happened when you got into bed with her?"

"I don't know . . ." She had begun to rock to and fro again, as she had done in the previous session, and she pressed her hands against her temples and closed her eyes. The look of desperation and vulnerability had returned to her face. "I don't want to talk about it. She'll find out about it if I talk about her . . . she'll get back at me. . . ."

"How could she find out?"

"She'll find out. . . ."

"There's only you and me here."

"I know, but . . ." She shook her head and looked up in terror. "She can sense things. She . . . can sense when I'm talking about her. She'll be waiting for me when I get back to my apartment. I'll . . . feel her in the room. She laughs at me, makes fun of me . . ." She glanced at me guardedly. "She's really there. I'm not hallucinating."

"Do you feel her presence now?"

"You mean here? Oh, no." She shook her head. "She

wouldn't come here. I feel safe here." Her body went through a sudden change. The terror melted from her eyes, her mouth fell slightly open, and she stopped rocking. "Actually, now that I think of it, I like it here," she said, looking about the room. "I like the way you've decorated your office." She reached out to touch the rug that had been hung on the wall beside her. I watched in amazement. "I like this rug here," she said. "That's a great idea, putting a rug on the wall. Maybe I'll do that in my apartment. It's very comforting." She patted the rug and smiled at me from the corner of her eyes, to make sure I knew what she meant by "comforting." What came to mind was a padded cell. I returned her smile, going along with her, thinking at the same time there was something unreal about her smile; that it was like a thin, transparent veneer covering layers of sadness. I also thought there was something conspiratorial about her smile, as though she already, after only two sessions, regarded me as a special, trusted confidant who would side with her against her mother and other evil forces in the world. "You know, I never really took a good look at your office," she said, and her eyes followed the oriental pattern of the rug down to the floor, where it was met by another oriental rug of similar design. She leaned down and touched the nap of the rug with her fingers, pressing her face against it to study the details. Then she sat up and took in a small oak desk chair, the leather sofa against the far wall, the oil paintings and wood carvings on the wall behind the sofa, the diplomas on the wall behind the oak desk, and the window beyond the desk that overlooked the courtyard. "Where did you get that desk?" she asked, as though she had known me for a long time. "Is it antique?"

"What are your thoughts about it?"

"I don't know. I always liked oak." She looked down. "I'm avoiding, aren't I?"

"It would seem so." She was avoiding, but I did not feel concerned. It was to be expected, I thought, after the way she had opened herself up to me during our first session. I figured she needed to pull back now and make sure she was safe, and perhaps show more of her "good" side. In fact, I felt as though I were seated in a balcony watching a performance on the floor below—like a parent watching a child—and it was easy for me to sit back and enjoy it. "What are you avoiding?" I asked in a casual voice.

"Talking about my childhood."

"You don't have to talk about it. You can talk about anything."

"I don't mind. I know I should. It's just . . . could you ask me some more questions?"

"How many brothers and sisters do you have?"

"Gobs." Her eyes rolled back. "There were seven of us in all. Four sisters and three brothers."

"Were you the oldest?"

"No, I was the second oldest. I had an older sister, Karen, but she mostly lived with my grandmother, who was kind of the matriarch of the family. My older sister was very beautiful, and my grandmother wanted to—as she put it—'raise her right.' She always thought my mother had married beneath her. You see, my mother's side of the family is English, Protestant—WASP—and my father is Scottish Catholic. There was always a lot of trouble about that in our house. My parents were always fighting over whether I should go to Catholic or Protestant churches." She spoke more freely now, glancing up at me now and then to see if I was listening. "Actually, it was my father and my grandmother who fought the most. They hated each other. My grandmother, well, she hated men, and my father hated women. But she was much stronger and she turned my older sister against him. Every time Karen came home my father and she would have it out. He kept telling her she was uppity like her grandmother and she'd criticize his table manners or whatever and they'd yell at each other and she'd walk out of the room in a huff. She was so beautiful as a little girl, my older sister. She was a child model. My grandmother took her around to the modeling agencies when she was still a baby. She made a lot of money. A *lot* of money. She was a Gerber baby. Did you ever see the old Gerber commercials on TV? You probably did. They were on all the time. Anyway, I think I got off the track. What was your question?" She glanced up with a sheepish grin. "Oh, yes, you wanted to know if I was the oldest. Actually, in effect, I *was* the oldest, so your sense of it was right. Karen was hardly ever around. In fact, I remember my father used to call me Little Mother because I was always taking care of things. I had to do most of the cooking and cleaning and taking care of my younger siblings. My mother was always . . . you know . . . drunk. She used to call me Prissy Pants. I don't know why. I guess she thought I was too proud. She never wanted any of us to be uppity. Neither did my father.

"Sometimes I get really sad now when I think about my mother." She looked up wistfully. "After she gave up dancing, all she did was get pregnant. One kid after another. She just let herself go. There was nothing I, or anybody, could do about it. Although I tried. I was always helping my father find and throw out her whisky bottles. But that's another story. Anyway. Did I answer your question? Wow. And I didn't want to talk about my childhood."

"How did it feel to talk about it?"

"All right, I guess."

"Do you feel afraid your mother will be waiting for you at your apartment?"

"No." She shook her head. "Not at all."

"Why are you smiling?"

"Actually, I was thinking . . . maybe I'd better not say what I was thinking." She smiled shyly, blushing.

"Why not?" I sat forward in my chair, thinking about how her mood had changed from the first session, about how it had fluctuated during the present one, about the name her mother had called her when she was a child, about her "performance," and about the blush that now came over her. I had a vision of her as a spunky three-year-old, enduring the molestations of this obviously disturbed mother, and felt a certain awe about what she'd endured. "Why can't you tell me what you're thinking?" I asked.

"Because it might jinx it."

"Jinx what? The therapy?"

"Yes . . . oh, well." She sighed. Her smile widened a bit, and there was that conspiratorial look. "I was thinking . . . I have a feeling something good will come of this." Her blush warmed the room.

3

S HE WALKED in and went right to her place in the corner without a word, folding her legs beneath her, Indian style. She was wearing the usual faded jeans and white, short-sleeved cotton blouse, but the blouse had paint smudges on it. Her hair was in pigtails, with light blue clips at the ends that brought out the blue in her eyes, and her thick orange braids, together with her pink freckles, made her look like a Raggedy Ann doll. A smile was at the edges of her lips.

"I've been doing some art work," she said. "I brought it in. I hope you don't mind." She held up a manila envelope.

"Of course not."

She took out about twenty-five sheets of thick art paper she had painted with acrylics. I sat in my chair looking on as she spread them out before her. Should I join her on the floor? I wondered. Or should I have her hand them to me so I can look at them in my chair? What will it mean to her if I join her on the floor? Will she see it as an act of seduction or submission? Or will she view it as an act of flexibility? With someone less depressed, less panic-stricken, less needy, I might have asked these questions out loud, but with someone like Jennifer, whose toleration for frustration was low, I decided to keep them to myself.

"Did you just do these?" I asked, getting down beside her.

"Yes. I've been working on them all day."

"Wonderful."

"Would you like to see them?"

"Of course."

She flicked the pigtails back and laid the stack of sheets in front of me, smiling impishly. She was feeling joyful today. She was quite pleased, she told me later, that I joined her on the floor. Her other therapist would never have sat on the floor with her. "Here they are," she said, and there was much more energy in her voice and in her movement than ever before, although there was an undertone of sadness and a certain clumsiness. "They're not very good. They're sort of . . . visual free associations. Actually, I think they're pretty depressing." She giggled nervously, sitting up all at once, and as she did so her head jerked backward and banged into the wall behind her. She did not seem to notice.

"Are you all right?"

"Oh, yes." She giggled embarrassingly.

"You seem amused by the fact that your paintings are so depressing."

"I guess maybe it's that *they're* depressing, but *I'm* not. Actually, I feel kind of good today."

"Great." She smiled in her conspiratorial way, and I returned her smile, thinking that she had almost completely dissociated herself from her depression and rage. Indeed, her dissociation was so great that she had smashed her head into the wall and hardly noticed it. I considered pointing out to her this evidence of how she was cut off from her feelings but decided against it. She needed to feel warm and safe for a while with her new idealized father-surrogate. Anyway, the paintings offered an indirect way of intervening. "Yes," I said, "there is a lot of depression in your work."

"Tell me about it." She chuckled again.

I turned the paintings over one at a time. They were full of red, brown, and black symbols—lines, circles, X's—done hastily with the fingers rather than a brush. A few were more figurative. One contained what looked like a monorail, with red droplets scattered here and there about the track. Another had a sad-looking face drawn in red and crossed out in black. Another showed a black volcano with red and brown lava, and deep down within the trunk of the volcano a deposit of yellowish matter. Still another —the most carefully executed of all—was comprised of red, black, and brown stripes with seven circles running across it.

"Which painting do you feel most drawn to?" I asked.

"What do you mean? Which one do I like?"

"No, which one draws your attention?"

"Oh. That one." It was the picture of the volcano.

"What do you see in it?"

"It's me. I'm about to explode."

"Is that the way you feel? You feel like exploding?"

"Usually I do. Not today, but usually I do."

"Then the lava is your anger?"

"Yes. And the black of the volcano is the depression that contains my rage." She smiled, proud of her professional insight. After all, she'd been exposed to enough of it.

"I see. And what is this yellow stuff deep inside the volcano?"

"I don't know. Do you?"

"Perhaps it's your tender feelings."

"How did you know? That's it, that's what it is!"

"So in order to get to your tender feelings, you'd have to explode first?"

"I guess so. But . . . I'm afraid to explode. I want to but I'm afraid of it."

"What are you afraid of?"

"I'm afraid I'd lose control. I'd be overwhelmed. I'd go crazy . . . and wouldn't come back."

"Perhaps if you found a safe place to explode you could do it and come back."

"You think so?"

She looked down at the paintings and began turning

them over, stopping to gaze ruefully at the one in which the face had been crossed out.

"Why did you cross out that face?"

"I don't know."

She kept going through the stack.

"What other painting are you drawn to?"

"I don't want to say."

"How come?"

"This one," she said, pulling one from beneath the pack. It was the one that looked like a monorail. It had a thick black line running up the middle, with short red lines forming crossbeams along the way. Bright red droplets were scattered at the bottom of the page.

"What does it say to you?"

"It's embarrassing."

"That's all the more reason you should talk about it."

"The black line is my arm. The red marks"—she grimaced—"are cuts in my arm. And these are drops of blood." She looked at me apologetically. "Sometimes when I'm feeling depressed I cut myself. I don't know why."

"How do you do that?"

"With a razor."

"May I take a look?"

"Why?"

"I'd just like to see how much damage you've done to yourself."

"I'm embarrassed."

"All right. Maybe some other time."

"Oh, well." She sighed. "You might as well see it. After all, you are my therapist." Again, as in the previous two sessions, I had the feeling of being given some rare privilege, of being let in on something mysterious and exclusive. She held out her left forearm, gazing at me with anticipation. I inspected the arm and tried not to show the feeling of sadness that came over me. The arm was covered with grooves from the wrist to the inside of the elbow. It looked like a miniature plowfield.

During the short time I had been practicing, I had known only two other patients who were physically self-destructive, one who burned herself with cigarettes and another who cut himself. Neither had been as destructive as Jennifer. I had never seen an arm like hers. There must have been thirty grooves in the left arm alone, and I noticed more on the right arm, which she held back. I gazed, mesmerized, at the arm, felt a chill on the back of my neck, and recalled a time when in a fit of anger I had smashed my fist into a desk and broken a bone in my hand. In some strange way, I had been proud of that wound, displaying it jokingly to friends. I recalled another time when my mother had flung a glass bowl at my father, causing a deep gash in his forehead, and my father had socked her in the eye. For days afterward she had shown everyone her black eye, as though it were a badge of courage. I realized in that moment, on both an emotional and intellectual level, what Jennifer was trying to tell me without telling me . . . her paintings were coded messages about her psychological state, and her arms were the proud vestiges of her suffering.

"You must have been pretty depressed." I looked at her.

"Here's my favorite," she said, quickly pulling out another painting. She saw that I was touched by her arm, and she looked embarrassed. She wanted me to care about her but not too much. She turned to the next painting, the one with seven interconnecting circles running across the page, each painted in a different color: red, brown, blue, yellow, green, orange, pink. "What do you think of this one?" she asked cheerfully.

"You don't want to talk about your arm?"

"Not really. What do you think of this one?"

"What do you see in it?"

"I see seven circles."

"What do they mean?"

"Seven people."

"Do you know them?"

"Yes." She giggled again, and her head jerked back, but this time it did not hit the wall behind her. She flicked back her pigtails. "Oh, yes, I know them well."

"Tell me about them."

"Some other time."

"Some other time?"

She flashed a coy smile. The smile said she liked me but she did not think I was ready to learn certain things. "Therapists pretend they don't make judgments," she said, "even when they do." She looked away from me, down at the painting.

I studied the seven circles to find the answer to her mystery for myself, but she quickly turned the paper over. We looked at the other paintings and she giggled a lot in a somewhat spastic way and seemed very cheery.

4

"I DON'T know what to say. . . ."

"Say whatever comes to your mind."

"Nothing's coming to my mind."

She was sitting on the floor again, her gaze downward, her jaw tight, her body arched and trembling. When she spoke, she did so with a great effort. She said later that at such times she felt as if some inner demon were holding on to her diaphragm and sucking air from her lungs. She sat frozen in place, even paler than usual. Her skin was completely without color and her hair, worn in a ponytail again, was dry and wiry, as though she had not washed it for days.

"You look upset," I said.

She nodded.

"Did something happen over the weekend?"

"I don't know. Yes." She looked up tiredly. "I went to . . . Pennsylvania to see my parents. They live outside Philadelphia . . . they . . . my mother . . ."

"Go on."

"Nothing really." She rocked to and fro and the pupils of her eyes seemed larger than usual, gawking out from her pale face like cat's eyes. "My mother said . . ." She paused to take in a deep breath and let it out slowly. "She said I was oversensitive."

"And that upset you?"

"Yes. I don't know why. I always seem to fly into a rage when she says that to me. It seems like such a little thing, I know. . . ." She looked meekly up into my eyes as though ashamed of being alive. "I started screaming at her. I was screaming and screaming. It was strange. I felt as if I were in some dark tunnel, screaming out of some dark tunnel. Then I blacked out. Sometimes I do that." She looked at me and I nodded. "Sometimes I can't remember whole periods of time. One moment I was screaming at my mother, and the next I was on the bus heading back, to New York. I didn't know . . . how I got on the bus."

"Why did your mother tell you you were oversensitive?"

"She was giving me advice. She does that a lot. She's always telling me I'm too thin, that I should eat this or that. I said I liked the way I looked but she wouldn't stop. She never lets up until I get angry. Then when I get angry, when I got angry and told her to mind her own business, she said I was oversensitive . . . and that's why I hadn't been able to make it as a dancer."

"But you *did* make it as a dancer."

"She doesn't think so. She . . . thinks I couldn't handle success. She thinks I'm a failure. Maybe she's right."

"So you started screaming at her?"

"Yes . . . I wanted . . . I wanted to kill her."

"Do you still feel like killing her?"

"I don't know . . . yes. . . ."

I had been studying her body language since she walked in and I saw that her rage was at the surface. Now I paused for a moment to try to decide what approach to take. I had been trained in both analytic and active therapy techniques and was still trying to figure out how and when to integrate them; it was a matter of finding my own therapeutic style. I was aware that many orthodox analysts felt that analytic and active techniques should never be combined, and they would cite the failed attempts of Ferenczi and others as proofs of their position. But those who had worked with more narcissistic patients—analysts such as Balint, Searles, Fromm-Reichmann, and Spotnitz

—generally used an eclectic approach. Each had to discover for himself how to do it, because there was no chart to follow. Even Freud had once noted that although psychoanalysis had proved to be the only method suited to his "individuality," he could not deny that "a physician quite differently constituted might feel impelled to adopt a different attitude toward his patients and toward the task before him."

I thought of all this and looked pointedly at Jennifer. "Would you like to do an experiential exercise?"

"What do you mean?"

I stood up and pulled an old wooden tennis racket from behind my desk. "Take this racket, hold it in both your hands like this, and hit the pillows of the sofa with it. I'll show you how." I gave the sofa a hard whack, letting out a grunt. "Come on, stand up. It'll do you good."

"I'm scared." She stood up, holding the racket limply at her side.

"Of what?"

"Of . . . losing control. . . ."

"Take a risk. I'm right here."

"I don't know." She stared at the sofa and her expression slowly changed. Her eyes widened and a small gleeful smile lit up her face. "You want me to hit the sofa?" she asked in a challenging, angry voice. "That's what you want me to do?" I nodded. "All right. I'll hit the sofa." She hoisted the racket above her head and brought it down with a loud clap. I watched her with my mouth slightly open, marveling at the abrupt change in her personality. I knew her rage was there, but I had expected more resistance. She brought the racket down again with all her might, smiling all the while like someone possessed. Then she snapped into a higher gear, plunged into the exercise, and flung the racket down three, four, five, six times in a noisy flurry. I was about to remind her to make a sound when I heard a crack. The racket had broken in half.

"I'm . . . sorry. . . ." She apologetically handed me the racket, looking flustered, as though unable to remember what had just happened.

"It's okay." I tossed the racket on top of my desk. "Don't worry about it."

"I'll pay for it, of course."

"It was only a cheap racket. I've got another at home."

"I'm sorry . . . I really am."

"Hey, you're pretty strong. It must be that volcano inside you."

"Yes, the volcano." She smiled with restrained pleasure, gazing at the racket with fondness. "Has anybody ever broken a racket before?"

"No, you're the first."

"Really?" She gazed at the racket. "I can't believe I broke it."

"It *is* pretty amazing."

"It was strange. . . .While I was hitting I felt weird, like . . . like it wasn't me who was hitting . . . like somebody else had taken over. . . ." She sat down on the floor again. The smile faded and was replaced by a distant gleam. "Sometimes . . . sometimes I think I don't know myself at all."

"What were you thinking when you were hitting?"

"I don't know."

I leaned toward her and sighed, wondering what it would take to open her up. "You know, Jennifer, I really care about you," I said, letting the words sink in, looking at her not just with my eyes but with my whole self. She kept her face hidden. "I feel a sense of urgency about your situation," I continued in a deliberate tone of voice. "I can see you're holding on to a lot of stuff. I think it would be very important for your therapy if you could talk about what you were thinking, what you were remembering while you were hitting."

"I was thinking about my mother." Her eyes were

fixed on the floor. "I was remembering . . . the long belt. . . ."

"The long belt?"

"She used to make us scrub the living room floor, all of us children. She'd sit in the middle of the room on her rocking chair with the long belt in one hand and a pint of whisky in the other."

"What do you mean by the long belt?"

"She would tie two or three narrow leather belts together."

"Like a homemade whip? It sounds like something out of Dickens." I shook my head, wondering for the first time if she was exaggerating.

"You don't believe me," she said with resignation.

"I believe you. I'm just shocked. What would she do, hit you with the whip if you didn't scrub properly?"

"Sometimes. . . ." She had begun to rock to and fro again. "Do I have to talk about this? . . . I don't see what good it will do. . . ."

"And your father?" I pressed. "Did he know about this?"

She did not answer. She was retreating, her body turned away; she looked nervously out the window. I started to feel panicky, then angry, then impatient, without knowing why. I had an impulse to grab her and shake her. Then I realized this was the countertransference she had induced. I had said one wrong thing—about Dickens—and she was ready to bolt. In those early days of doing therapy I used to feel this panic a lot. "Jennifer," I said, "I do believe you. It sounded a little melodramatic at first, about the whip and scrubbing the floor, but I *do* believe you." She kept gazing across the room. "Did your father know she did this?"

She sighed. Finally a barely audible "no" came out.

"You never told him?"

"He didn't want to know anything. . . . If I tried to tell him anything, he'd say I was making it up or yell at me, and then later my mother would get back at me for telling him. I remember one time I tried to tell him about the dog, and he wouldn't listen. He just said, 'You shouldn't talk about your mother that way.' "

"About the dog? What dog?"

"There was this dog . . . this dog who came to our house one day and his mouth was foamy, and my mother said to me, 'Go out and give that dog some water. I think he's thirsty. Give him some water.' So I went out and put a tray of water near the dog and he started chasing me. . . . Then I couldn't get back into the house. My mother had latched the door . . . she was smiling. . . . She had a smile on her face, and my little sister . . . was screaming. Martha was scared to death. But I was calm . . . I don't know why, but I was calm. I didn't scream or cry or anything."

"What did you do?"

"I . . . ran around and came in through the front door."

"How old were you then?"

"About six or seven, I think."

"And when you told your father about it he cautioned you not to talk about your mother that way?"

"Yes. . . . He always told me, 'You should love your mother. Your mother has had a rough life and you should love her.' Whenever I tried to tell him anything, he'd get angry at me. He'd lose his temper and yank all the kids out of bed and spank them one by one . . . then he'd go in my mother's room and yank her out of bed and beat her. . . . He had a terrible temper. I never told him anything. I was expected to take care of her. If I said anything, things got worse . . . I just tried to handle it myself. . . .

"I remember once she was running around with a knife . . . a butcher's knife . . . and I sent all the other kids outside and tried to get her to give me the knife. . . ." Her eyes were darting right, then left.

"Did she give it to you?"

"She . . . stabbed me in the hand. . . ."

"How old were you then?"

"About seven or eight. I think."

"And you never told your father about that either?"

"No."

"What about her sexual abuse? Did you ever tell him about that?"

"No. I never told him anything . . . and I never told *anybody* about that. Not even my brothers or sisters. I was . . . ashamed. It was like a secret between my mother and me. . . . It was . . ." She shook her head slowly, grimacing. "It was a horrible secret."

"What happened?"

"I don't want to talk about it."

"Is it still a secret?"

"No. It's not a secret now." She shook her head slowly, with determination. "I don't want it to be a secret anymore."

"How often did it occur?"

". . . Several times a week. . . ."

"And it started when you were three, you said?"

". . . Yes. . . ."

"What would she do?"

"I . . . can't remember. . . ." She shut her eyes tight. "She . . . she used to make me lie beside her and . . . and . . . she'd . . ."

"What?"

"She'd . . . fondle me. . . . I really don't want to think about this. . . ."

"Where would she fondle you?"

"Sometimes . . . sometimes . . . she'd stick . . . fingers . . . bottles . . ."

"Bottles?"

". . . whisky bottles. . . ." Her breath came shallow and quick. "I think . . . I think she'd hold her hand over my mouth so I couldn't scream. . . . Sometimes I'd bleed. . . . I didn't know what was happening. . . . I

. . . pretended I wasn't there. . . ." A sob welled to the surface and she sucked in her breath. "I can't," she said. "I can't." Her body stiffened. It was as if she were actually going through the experience again at that moment, and was in danger of annihilation. To cry meant to weaken, to give in to the annihilation. She held on to her breath as long as she could, then let out a little whimper, a sob, and a flood of sobs and tears. Then she caught herself again, held her breath for a moment, and a new flood erupted. She struggled with these feelings, wincing in pain, turning her head this way and that, and I looked on feeling her pain.

I was stunned. A murderous rage had taken possession of me and I could not speak. I had a fantasy of driving up to her parents' house that evening and telling them off. I saw myself beating up both of them with a tennis racket.

"It's all right," I finally said. "It's all right."

"I shouldn't have talked about her," she muttered between sobs. "I really shouldn't have . . . she'll find out. . . ." She sobbed some more, but she would not let herself cry. Not yet.

SESSION

5

S HE HELD out a large yellow mum, smiling shyly. "This is for you."

I took it in both hands and sniffed it. "Thank you. It's beautiful. To what do I owe this honor?" I asked, putting the mum in a vase on the windowsill.

"You should get lots of flowers," she said, waltzing into the room.

"I should? How come?"

"Just because." She smiled to herself. "Because you're you."

She went to the window to look into the courtyard. A breeze caught her hair, which today was worn loosely around the shoulders and had a yellowish hue that matched the color of the mum. She rested her hands on the windowsill and leaned out into the air, her firm dancer's hips protruding and her well-defined legs bare beneath a short skirt. I watched her admiringly, amazed at the dramatic change in mood, and had an impulse to embrace her.

Both of us were in high spirits. It was one of those sunny but cool mornings when the scent of newly mowed grass, upturned roots, and dank soil turned over in the sun seems to penetrate your being. It was a lovely day but I knew as well as she that her buoyant mood was not just due to the weather.

"The place looks different today, larger," she said, whirling around, the secret smile on her lips, her hands clasped behind her back. She glanced at me, and then down at my brown corduroy jacket and red polka-dot tie. "I could do a dance here."

"Why don't you?"

"I'm not quite ready yet. Someday." She whirled once more and came to rest in the chair, where she slid her palms along the armrests and crossed her legs with a flourish. "I have nothing to talk about today. Everything's been going well." She arranged the hem of her skirt so that it covered her knees. It was the first time she had worn a skirt. "What shall we talk about?"

"Whatever you like."

"Whatever I like? Hmmmmm."

I smiled at her and she averted her eyes. I had thought about her constantly since our last session, touched by the things she had recalled and concerned that I had pushed her too hard. In fact, I had half-expected her not to show up today. But here she was, dancing around my office. "You're in good spirits today," I said.

"I've been feeling that way since our last session."

"What was it about the last session?"

"I think it was when you said you cared about me." She glanced up bashfully. "That really meant a lot to me."

"How come?"

"I don't know. Anyway, I just wanted you to know I care about you too. That's why I brought you something. I was a little afraid about giving you the mum, though."

"Why?"

"I didn't want to lead you on. I'm afraid I'd be responsible . . . in case I . . . you know . . . do something self-destructive."

"What do you mean?"

"I guess I'm feeling ambivalent. I want you to care about me—and then I don't want you to. I'm afraid if you care about me too much you'll be hurt if I kill myself. I don't want you to think that because I gave you the flower I'm making some kind of commitment. Am I making sense?"

"Yes, you're making sense."

"Then you understand what I'm saying?"

"I think so."

As a therapist I understood completely. As a therapist I was aware that she might have perceived my statement of caring as something more, to which she had now replied, demurely, with a caution. It also occurred to me that the flower was yellow—the color she had used for her tender feelings in her drawing of the volcano. I had told her she would have to explode before she could experience her tender feelings, and in the last session she *had* exploded to some extent. But she probably knew, as I did, that this explosion was only "a drop in the bucket." She had much rage left inside her.

As a therapist I understood that she had transferred her father onto me, and just as she had once protected her father from all the craziness that was happening at home, now she wanted to protect me from the craziness that was happening inside of her. Her ambivalence as to whether she wanted me to care about her was connected with conflicts about whether she wanted to make love to or kill her father, and the flower was a test to see if I would be strong enough to resist becoming overinvolved with her. Her mother had become overinvolved with her, as had her father. So had other therapists. She had a power and she knew about it and enjoyed it, but at the same time she also knew that the power had often led to her undoing.

As a therapist, I understood all this. As a man I found myself feeling excited and warmed by her. Sometimes, when she scrutinized me, I wondered if she saw through me, if she could see my need and longing; if she knew that I had my own anger toward women and toward my mother, that I, too, had a raw wound needing to be attended.

In those days I was still full of unresolved complexes; yet, having just graduated from an institute, I fancied that I had more or less completed my psychotherapeutic train-

ing. I did not realize then that the profession of psychotherapy requires its practitioners to undergo a lifetime psychotherapy, along with supervision and other training, in
order to insure that they have no blind spots that might get
in the way of doing therapy.

"You're afraid that giving me the flower might make
me expect something from you?" I said after a while, trying to keep my feelings out of it.

"Exactly." She let out a sigh, apparently comforted
by my understanding of her ambivalence. "It's just something I wanted to do."

"What do you think I might expect?"

"I don't know." She smiled the secret smile again. "So
what shall we talk about? Oh, I said that already. By the
way, you'll probably be interested in knowing that I heard
voices when I got home after the last session."

"Your mother's?"

"Yes."

"What did she say?"

"She was laughing because I talked about her. But it
was okay. It only lasted a little while, then she went
away."

"How'd you get rid of her?"

"I called up my friend Bonnie."

"Who's Bonnie?"

"She's this girl I met during my last stay at St. Elizabeth's. She's kind of like me. She also had taken an overdose of pills. Now we call each other whenever we're suicidal. We have a pact. I yell at her and she yells at me."

"So she yelled at you and you got rid of your
mother?"

"Sort of."

"Sounds good."

"Yes." She crossed her legs at the ankles and fixed her
skirt again, bringing her arms up lazily behind her head. "I
really don't have anything pressing to talk about."

"That's fine."

"Could we just chat today? Could we just have a light, friendly chat? We don't always have to get into heavy feelings, do we? Could we just have a nice chat today?"

"Certainly."

"Could we do that, just today?"

"Whatever you like. It's your session."

"Oh, good! I was afraid you'd want me to use the racket again, or talk about my mother. That's a relief." She sighed, half closing her eyes for a moment. Then she smiled and patted the armrests with her hands. "Let's just have a warm, friendly, light chat. Okay?"

SESSION

6

SHE WAS silent and still in the dark corner. Her eyes were gazing off, and the sunlight from the window made a ray across her mouth, which was slightly open.

"What's that?" I asked.

"What?" She glanced up, startled.

"On your arm."

"Oh . . . I . . . cut myself."

"Let me see." She held out her forearm and I inspected it. There was a fresh scab a few inches above the wrist. I looked at the scab and felt disappointed, but I asked, as though merely curious, "When did you do it?"

"Saturday night."

"Did something happen?"

"No. . . ." She gazed off. "I just . . . I couldn't stand it. . . ."

"Stand what?"

". . . Just . . . being alive . . . being . . ." A long sigh. "I don't know . . . sometimes . . . I wish . . ."

"You felt depressed?"

"Yes. Sometimes . . . everything feels so hopeless, so false, so empty. Sometimes I feel as if I'll always be this way . . . why bother?"

"Always be what way?"

"Sad . . . afraid . . . no good. . . ." She looked down and the ray of sunlight swept across her left eye which, held in relief, looked peculiarly large and still, as though she were waiting for a drop of eye medicine. "I just feel . . . worthless . . . nobody really cares about me . . . there's nothing to live for. . . ."

"I thought you felt *I* cared about you."

"Only because I pay you to care."

"That's not how you felt last session."

"I don't know how I felt last session. I only know how I feel now. . . . You care about me but you're a therapist, not a friend. . . ."

"So, if I'm a therapist, my caring is no good?"

"I didn't say that. . . ."

A sigh quivered out of her as she sat gazing off. I leaned toward her, wanting to be nearer to the source of her pain. I had expected that her mood would change, but not this soon.

"Jennifer, would you like to do an exercise?"

"No. . . ." She shook her head.

"What were you thinking about when you cut yourself?"

"Henrietta."

"Who's Henrietta?"

"She's . . . my dearest friend. . . . I haven't told you about her. I don't like to think about it."

"About what?"

"She's . . . she's in the hospital. . . . She has cancer. . . ." Her eyes were squinting back tears. "I don't want her to die. I don't know what I'll do if she dies. Oh, God. Oh, God, I don't want her to die. . . ." She rubbed her arms.

"How old is she?"

"Not old." There was resentment in her voice. "I mean, she's eighty, but she's always had so much beauty, so much zest, so much grace. . . . I called the hospital Saturday and they said they might have to amputate her leg. . . . Can you imagine what that would do to her, a former prima ballerina?" A cry came up from deep down and was immediately choked off. "I couldn't endure seeing her like that. I know I couldn't."

"Would you be talking about Henrietta Ross?" She

was the founder and principal choreographer of the Apple Company.

"Yes. . . ."

"I suppose you were close?"

"Close?" She spat the words out. "She discovered me when I was attending P.A."

"P.A.?"

"The High School of Performing Arts. She taught me everything I know about dance, about Labanotation, about professional ethics, about stage presence. She's always been there for me. We've traveled together, done workshops together for dance troupes all over the world. She's the only one . . . the only person who understands me. And now I'm losing her." She buried her face in her hands and took in several deep breaths. "I don't want her to die. Oh, God, don't let her die. . . ." She held her breath but a few sobs bubbled up as she rocked back and forth, hugging herself, looking out the window. The ray of light had moved away and her face was now in shadow. She looked sad and mysterious in the shadow.

As she continued to struggle with her tears, now and then putting out a phrase or a sob, I sat in my chair not looking at her, my eyes half closed, my stillness matching hers. I did not want to break into her reverie or draw attention to myself. I was tempted to tell her to "let it out," but my sense of her mood was that she would not do that today. Her emotions were in another place, a place where only certain actions in connection with certain people could unleash them. Perhaps if Henrietta herself had appeared in the office at that moment, the tears would have come. Otherwise, they would stay locked inside her, each tear symbolic of a "terrible" secret that must be kept from the world.

I was concerned, aware that she had pulled away from me. In contrast to the previous session, when I had felt a strong bond forming between us, today she seemed far away and virtually unreachable. For the first time I was really afraid of what she might do after she left my office. Toward the end of the session I said, "Jennifer, we're going to have to stop now. But I feel a little worried about you. Will you be all right?"

"I'll be all right." She made her way to the door.

"Jennifer?"

"Yes?" She stopped in the doorway.

"I just want you to know something." I spoke in a neutral way. "If you commit suicide, I won't be your therapist anymore." I grinned mischievously and raised my brows, hoping to reach the part of her that had formed the "conspiracy" with me.

She looked at me with surprise. Then a rueful laugh broke out. "That's true." She was almost smiling as she turned to go. "That's certainly something to think about."

IN THE HOSPITAL

"JENNIFER?" I called her on the phone the following Monday.

". . . yes. . . ." Her voice sounded as though it were floating in space.

"What's up? It's 4:25."

". . . I'm not coming in. . . ."

"What's going on?"

". . . not feeling very well. . . ."

"Are you suicidal?"

". . . yes. . . ."

"Jennifer, if you're suicidal, perhaps you ought to call your friend, Bonnie, and have her stay with you."

". . . I don't know. . . . I think maybe I should check myself in. . . ."

"Where?"

". . . St. Elizabeth's. . . ."

"Where you were before?"

". . . yes. . . ."

"Then maybe that's the thing to do. Go there right away, okay? And call me when you get there. If I don't hear from you within an hour or so, I'll have to call the police for assistance."

". . . yes. . . ."

I called her several times within the next two hours and got no answer, then tried to call the hospital, but got put on "hold" and left there. I was about to call the police when the phone rang.

"I'm here," she said. Her voice was calm but distant, her tone like that of a robot. "I'll probably be here for a week. I'll let you know when I get out. I still want to see you. Thanks for everything."

She was on my mind the rest of the week. I had by then already become overly involved with her, and could not wait to visit her.

She was on the eighth floor of a high white building—nestled between dark green lawns and gardens of English ivy and tulips of orange, purple and yellow—that overlooked the East River and the factories of Queens. As I walked up the sidewalk and into the lobby, I felt uneasy, concerned about how this visit might affect our therapeutic relationship, rationalizing that she was a special patient who had special needs. I remembered that her previous therapists had gotten overinvolved, but I did not think that was the case with me.

When she came drifting down the cool, marbled hallway, her pink terry-cloth robe flapping against her bare legs, looking like some forlorn waif, I felt something I had not felt before: pity. It was hard to look at her as she lowered herself into the velvet sofa. Drugs had snuffed out her suicidal impulses along with all her other feelings. I smiled through my sadness and she looked at me blankly, indifferently.

"I didn't expect you'd really visit me," she half-whispered. Her words echoed down the marble hallway. She was not really indifferent; I believed that deep down somewhere she felt grateful and truly surprised that I had come. Only one other therapist had ever taken the time to visit her in the hospital, and he had done so grudgingly. But she showed no feeling: the medication had done something to her facial muscles. "I really didn't expect it," she repeated.

"You asked me to."

"I know."

"Well, here I am." I grinned good-naturedly.

"Yes. Here you are."

There was a moment of awkwardness and she looked out the window at a barge that was stalled in the middle of the water. I followed her eyes out the window, then looked down at her knees, then up at the ceiling. I was sitting stiffly, hands in my pockets, self-consciously trying not to look self-conscious. She picked up my self-consciousness and began to feel the same way. She too began to squirm.

"It's quiet," I said.

"It is. Very quiet. At night you can hear the horns of the boats."

"And the view isn't bad either."

"Yes, it's one of the best hospitals in the city. If you're going to voluntarily commit yourself, this is the place to do it. It's the Ritz of loony bins." She smiled feebly.

Our eyes met for a moment. I looked away, not wanting her to see the sadness, or perhaps the pity, in my eyes. I have never felt comfortable in hospitals.

"How long do you think you'll be here?" I asked.

"Not long. They're pretty good about letting you go when you think you're ready. I'll probably get out in a few days. I'm over the crisis. Maybe I'll even be able to make my Tuesday appointment with you."

"There's no need to rush."

"I've been thinking . . . maybe I should do more hitting with your tennis racket."

"If you like."

"I really think I ought to, don't you?"

"It would probably be beneficial."

"I'm sure it would. Did you get a new racket yet?"

"Yes, I found one in a thrift shop."

"I'm sorry I broke the other one."

"You can break my rackets anytime if it helps you feel better." I smiled and her face brightened a bit. I was trying not to notice the peculiar smell from the Thorazine that came from her.

"It's nice of you to spend your Saturday afternoon visiting me. I'm sure you have other things to do."

"I do have some errands to run later this afternoon."

"Please don't let me keep you."

"Don't worry about it."

"Are you sure?"

"It's nothing. I just need to do some shopping."

"I'm really fine now. You don't have to stay on my account."

"No, it's okay, really."

"I do appreciate your coming."

"How are you feeling?"

"Not bad, considering." A frown was detectable around the eyes. "I have to take all this medicine that tires me out, but I'm not suicidal anymore. I have a nice room down the hall. Only three roommates."

"Just like the Ritz—and with a river view."

"Except at the Ritz they don't lock you in."

I looked out the window at the barge. It was still sitting there going nowhere. This visit, I thought, is going nowhere, but there's not much I can do or say while she's so heavily medicated. I decided I had stayed long enough to be polite.

"Are you sure I'm not keeping you?" she asked. I probably looked so uncomfortable she really wished I would leave.

"I'll stay a little while longer." I smiled politely.

"It was really considerate of you to come."

"I was in the neighborhood."

"I think I need to do more hitting with your racket. I'll try to make the Tuesday appointment, if that's all right with you." She gazed at me without emotion. "I promise not to break it this time."

S HE HAD taken root in my mind like some growing thing. I thought about her as soon as I woke up in the morning. I thought of her while doing therapy with other patients. I thought of her in the evenings while I watched the news on television. Recently divorced, I had not yet found a substitute for my ex-wife, and for some time I had spent my evenings brooding, locked in a state of mild depression; now Jennifer had awakened my interest in life, in work, and in the people around me; she had given a new meaning to my existence. It was gratifying to be so needed by someone. This was a reward of doing therapy.

I had been particularly struck by her stoicism during my hospital visit. Even while heavily medicated, I noted, she still kept her pride, and even when things were at their worst she was concerned about me—about whether or not I would get my errands done. At times I would let my thoughts take wing and I would lose sight of objectivity. At such times I would see only her talent, her intelligence, her beauty, her nobility, and other attributes she may or may not have had. In those days I would sometimes "fall in love" with certain patients and, as often happens in this state, begin idealizing the object of my affection. There would be a selective inattention (as Sullivan put it) to the psychopathological aspects of her personality, inattention, for example, to her father-transference and to the ambivalence she felt toward me—the negative component of which she warded off through appeasing behavior.

She had said to me at one point, when she had detected a tear in my eye, that I was strong enough to be vulnerable, unlike other therapists who pretended to be strong but were really fragile. I liked that. I thought of this often. But I did not think enough about her unconscious transference aims. On that level I was the good father whom she would charm into submission, draw into a conspiracy with her against mother, marry, and take, hand in hand, toward the sunrise. On that level much was expected of me; indeed, I was a matter of life or death to her.

Nor did I always properly assess the meaning of the various moods and personalities she presented to me in succeeding interviews. I had thought about it from time to time, but I had attributed her changes to a borderline character structure, to shifts in identification, to a weak ego that could not mediate between the harsh, menacing superego (introjected, I thought, from her mother) and the longings from her libidinal self. However, I was to find out what these changes meant in the next session.

She arrived a few minutes early on that "fateful" day, again holding out a flower—this time a red tulip. "For you."

"Again?" I took the tulip and put it in my vase, wondering if she had plucked it from St. Elizabeth's. "You're going to spoil me."

"It's just my way of saying thanks for coming to visit me."

She sat down on the chair somewhat stiffly. Her mood was dark again.

"Are you still on Thorazine?"

"Is it that noticeable?"

"You seem a bit muted."

"Yes, that's the way I feel. But I don't think I'm ready to go without it. Will it hurt the therapy if I'm on medication?"

"No, not really."

"I feel terrible about it. I don't like being on drugs but I'm scared not to be." She sat rigidly against the back of the chair, her face a chalky white. "I know I said I'd do some hitting with your racket but . . . I don't know if I'm ready yet."

"It's all right."

"Maybe in a week or so. . . ."

"Whenever you're ready."

"Thanks."

I smiled at her and she averted her eyes.

"Anyway, aside from the Thorazine, how are you feeling?"

"Depressed. Hopeless."

"What's the depression and hopelessness about?"

"It's a pessimistic feeling. A doomed feeling. It's always there, really. A feeling that I'm never going to be happy . . . never going to accept myself." She pressed her palms against her temples and closed her eyes. "Now I'm hearing a voice in my head. . . ."

"What does the voice say?"

"It says . . . I could be happy if I wanted to be. . . ."

"Then you have an optimistic part of you?"

"Yes . . . I guess . . . I'm confused. . . ."

"Let's do some role-playing. Be your optimistic self. Here, sit in this chair." I pushed a folding chair toward her. "Sit here and be your optimistic self." I wanted to try to break through the confusion.

"Sit in that chair?"

"Yes." I nodded emphatically and she slowly arose, eying the folding chair with suspicion.

"Sit in this chair?" She looked at me and I nodded again. She sat down tentatively. "Now what?"

"Talk to your pessimistic self."

"You want me to imagine my pessimistic self is sitting in the empty chair?"

"Yes."

She stared at the empty chair and the confused expression began to fade and a transformation occurred. It was the same kind of transformation I had witnessed previously when she was hitting with the racket. Now, as then, a small gleam appeared in her face, and her very features underwent a modification—her cheekbones protruded more, her jaw came out, and her eyes grew larger and stronger. Her posture also changed, and she sat upright with her head held straight and her eyes staring confidently and a bit disdainfully at the empty chair. When she spoke her voice was full and angry.

"You *could* be happy if you wanted to," she said to the empty chair. "All you need to do is stop feeling sorry for yourself. All you need to do is get back to work, stop moping around, stop putting yourself down all the time." She looked at me with the same contempt she had directed toward the chair. "Well? What now?"

"Tell her how you feel about her," I said.

"She disgusts me."

"Tell her."

"You disgust me. You have so much talent, so much potential, but you never do anything with it. I'm tired of seeing you sit around and whine about doom and gloom. I'm sick of your doom and gloom, and of your suicide attempts. I'm sick of your destructiveness. All you need to do is stop living in the past and get back to work. That's all. Just get back to work. I don't know what else to say to you."

I was amazed that Jennifer had such a strong personality inside her. I had begun to wonder what it meant about her character, and decided to pursue it. "So, you're Jennifer's optimistic self."

"That's right."

"Let's give you a name."

"I already have a name."

"You do? What is it?"

"Margaret."

"Oh, I see. Where did the name come from?"

"I've always had it."

She looked at me with amusement flickering in her hardened gaze. I stared back with rising curiosity.

"Do you mean you were named Margaret when you were born?"

"In a sense."

"It's your middle name?"

"It's Jennifer's middle name."

"Oh. So when you're feeling optimistic, you think of yourself as Margaret. And when you're feeling pessimistic, you think of yourself as Jennifer."

"No, I always think of myself as Margaret."

"Always?"

"That's right."

"I don't understand."

"I know." She flashed a superior smile.

"Would you mind explaining."

"I'm not Jennifer. Never have been. I'm Margaret. We're two different people."

"Then you're saying you have two different personalities?"

"Actually, there are seven of us."

"Seven. I see. And do the others have names as well?"

"Of course."

"Then what you're saying is . . . that you have multiple personalities?"

"Yes, being a shrink, you'd put it that way." She smiled condescendingly, meeting my stare with no flinching. "You shrinks need your labels."

"How would you put it?"

"I'd say there are seven people."

"And you all share the same body?"

"That's right."

"And who are the others? What are their names?"

"Besides Jennifer and me there are: Mildred, Tom, Jess, Jenny, and Mary."

"Tom? One of the personalities is a man?"

"A boy."

"How old is he?"

"Tom's nine. He's very angry."

"At his mother?"

"No, his father. Jennifer's the one who has most of the anger at our mother."

"I see. And what are the others like?"

"Well, there's Jenny. She's the youngest; she's six. She's a really good kid, very smart. Then there's Jess. She claims she's only twenty-four. She likes to have fun."

"Fun? What do you mean?"

"I suppose you'd say she was a nymphomaniac. She likes to go to bars and pick up men. She's not into taking responsibility for herself, and I'm always having to straighten up her messes. She and I don't get along too well."

"Go on. What about the others?"

"Mildred's the writer and intellectual. She's writing a book. She's the one who went to college. Then there's Mary, who was born in England but raised in Jennifer's house."

"How old are they?"

"Mildred and Mary and I are all the same age, twenty-nine." She looked at him. "So?"

"And you all know about each other? You're all aware of each other's existence?"

"No, not all of us. I know everything about everybody. The others know what they want to know."

"And what about Jennifer? Does she know about all of you?"

"Sort of. She knows we exist, but she tries to hide it from herself."

"Is she aware of what's going on right now?"

"No."

"Does your other therapist know about you?"

"No. Nobody else knows. I tried to tell him who I was once, but he thought I was delusional. He diagnosed us as manic-depressive."

Us? I must have had a strange expression as it finally dawned on me that she was a multiple. I had never encountered a multiple before. I had read about them in books and seen movies about them, but I had never actually been exposed to one, not even during my internship at Bellevue. Since then I have seen other multiples, as well as an array of other exotic character formations. But nothing can compare with the first encounter with a multiple.

I understood immediately why centuries ago people like Jennifer were thought to be possessed. It was truly uncanny. The atmosphere in the room seemed to jump with her personality change, and I was intensely aware of the two of us, face to face, all alone with one another in that moment. It was a turning point for me, and it was also a turning point for her, a coming out of the psychic closet.

For several moments I simply stared at her, and she looked back with a wry grin. "Well," I said after I had snapped out of my reverie and glanced at my watch, "perhaps I'd better talk with Jennifer."

"That's up to you," Margaret replied. She eyed me with cynicism, amused by my obvious bewilderment. "You're the shrink."

"Would you mind changing chairs again?" I asked.

She shrugged, rolled back her eyes, and grudgingly changed chairs. Her eyes went sad and her brows furrowed and her arms clung to herself once more. Then her body began rocking to and fro. "I'm . . . confused," came a small voice, Jennifer's voice.

"Jennifer?"

"Yes?" She looked up, frightened, apologetic.

"What are you confused about?"

"I'm not sure what just happened."

"You were role-playing. I asked you to play your pessimistic and optimistic selves."

"Yes, I remember that."

"You don't remember talking to me as Margaret?"

"No . . . I don't remember anything."

"Do you know who Margaret is?"

"I hear her voice . . . in my head . . . sometimes."

She glanced about the room as though she had just landed there in a time machine. I studied her, observing the physical changes in her. Her face had grown softer, the cheekbones had receded, the jaw was less tense. The overall hardness had given way to vulnerability.

"Are you aware," I said calmly, "that you have multiple personalities?"

"I don't know . . . what do you mean? . . ."

"Are you aware of the other personalities inside you —Margaret, Jenny, Tom, and the others?"

"I don't know. . . . I feel confused. . . ."

"Then you really didn't hear anything that Margaret was saying to me just now?"

"No. I feel as though I just woke up . . . as though I just awoke from a deep sleep."

"But you weren't asleep, Jennifer. You were just sitting in that chair over there." I pointed to the now-empty chair. "You were talking to me as Margaret." I looked at her. "You don't remember anything?"

"I don't know. . . ."

"Jennifer?"

She shook her head, slowly, in a daze.

"You are were sitting right there."

"I don't know . . . I really . . . don't know. . . . I'm . . . confused. . . ."

THE THERAPIST'S JOURNAL

GOING TO have to keep a more detailed diary after the revelations of the last few days. It's like I've been catapulted into another sphere of life. Each day brings a new surprise. Imagine, a multiple personality in my first year of practice. Feel so lucky, but also guilty about feeling lucky. Therapists aren't supposed to be thrilled by patients. That's called countertransference. Well, if this is countertransference, let me bask in its glory for a while. I've never felt so alive.

No, I must calm down. Freud says that a therapist's attitude toward a patient should be like that of a surgeon's. When the surgeon is preparing to make a cut across the patient's body, he's not thinking about the patient's feelings, otherwise he couldn't make the cut. "The more plainly the analyst lets it be seen that he is proof against every temptation," Freud says, "the more readily will he be able to extract from the situation its analytic content." Must calm down, not give in to the temptation to revel in my feelings about Jennifer. On the other hand, to deny the feelings would be equally destructive; feelings denied always get acted out one way or another. Must allow myself to have them, yet not let them control me or get in the way of the therapy. Must use them to understand how she's affecting me, and what she's feeling herself. If I'm feeling lucky, then she must be experiencing a corresponding feeling of making me lucky. If I'm feeling tempted, then she must on some level be wanting to tempt me. If I'm feeling guilty, there's probably a desire to make me feel guilty. What can I extract from the analytic content?

As I ponder these questions, I continue to be amazed by Margaret. Haven't seen Jennifer for three sessions, not since Margaret made her first appearance. Must be some kind of hypnotic communication. Multiples very suggestible. Once Margaret got the message that I was excited by her emergence, she continued to appear. Pretends she hates me, but I don't think she really does, at least not entirely. There's also a grudging admiration.

It's fascinating. She really is a different person from Jennifer. No actress could possibly do this. An actress would always have a part of herself observing what the other part was doing—an observing ego. But when Jennifer becomes Margaret there's a complete dissociation. No observing ego. Jennifer—the "ego" of her seven personalities—is unconscious, unaware of what's happening. The change in personality is complete from the inside out. Not only is her personality different, but even the shape of her body and face. It seems there may be a completely different organization with each personality. Jennifer apparently identifies closely with her mother, while Margaret identifies with the father. At the same time Jennifer's animosity is strongest toward her mother, while Margaret's is strongest against her father. The identification in each case is with the hated (but on some level admired) object: the aggressor.

Margaret's most predominant character trait may be her feistiness. Today she *strode* in with a dark sulky glare in her eyes. Hair severely pulled back in a bun. Red shorts. Low-neckline blouse. She plopped down on the chair with the posture of a man, legs spread out, hands on hips. Silently stared at me until I said something.

"You're not going to sit on the floor today?"

"Nope."

I looked at her. She glared. Glare so strong I had to look away.

"Are we having a staring contest?"

"If you say so."

"Feisty, aren't you?"

"I'm not scared of you, if that's what you mean."

"You must be Margaret today."

"You don't say."

"Do I detect a bit of sarcasm?"

"I didn't think you'd be smart enough to tell who I was."

She leaned back, her arms resting on the arms of the chair, opening and closing her legs, slowly, glaring at me. I looked down at her legs. They were nice legs to look at, but it was distracting. Could have ignored them, but felt she was analytic enough to hear an interpretation. Assumed she was doing it as a provocation to defend against her feelings of fear. Women often use their sexuality to take control of the situation. But it's very delicate to interpret their sexual language, because they usually deny it, particularly if they're hysterical.

"Why are you looking at my legs?" she asked.

"They're very seductive."

"Why, because I'm wearing shorts?"

"That and because of the way you're sitting and moving them."

"I think *you're* seductive."

"How am I seductive?"

"The way you're sitting."

I looked down at myself. I was seated spread-legged in my chair, the way I often sit. Hadn't ever thought of it as seductive. Supposed it probably was. When I looked up at her a little sheepishly, she had a grin of triumph. "That's interesting," I said. "I never thought of this posture as seductive."

"Well, it is."

"Thanks for letting me know." I crossed my legs. "Is this less seductive?"

"I suppose. I don't really care, to tell you the truth."

She continued to open and close her legs. I sat back to consider a new approach. Kept looking at her legs.

"There is a slight difference, though," I said.

"What's that?"

"You're wearing shorts and I'm not."

"I'm wearing shorts because it's summer and that's what I feel most comfortable in. If you don't want me to wear shorts, just say so. It's your office."

"I'm sorry. I've made you angry."

"I'm not angry at you."

"Somebody else?"

"I'm angry that I can't dress how I want to and be how I want to without people making an issue of it."

"People?"

"Yes, people. Like my neighbor, the Chinaman."

"What about the Chinaman?"

"He's always gawking at me. He lives across the alley and he can see into my living room from his bathroom window."

"So?"

"So, I don't wear any clothes on hot days like today. I can't afford an air conditioner so I walk around nude. Is that a crime? And every time I turn around the Chinaman is gawking at me from his bathroom window. I hope the bastard gets an eyeful."

"So, do you think I'm like this Chinaman? Gawking at you?"

"Right."

"And you wish I'd let you be?"

"Precisely."

"Is that also how Jennifer feels? Does she wish I'd let her be?"

"Jennifer's scared of you."

"What does that mean?"

"She wants to please you."

"So she doesn't want me to let her be?"

"I don't know. You'll have to ask her."

"You said you knew about all the other personalities."

"I do. But I don't feel like talking about Jennifer."

"Do you feel like talking about the other personalities?"

"Nope."

"How come?"

"I just don't."

"Then what would you like to talk about?"

"Nothing." She folded her arms and glared at me. "I'm not here to do therapy. I don't need therapy."

"Then why did you come?"

"Somebody had to."

"Why didn't Jennifer come in?"

"She's too depressed."

She yawned. Opened her legs a bit wider. I smiled, thinking how incredible she was, amazed that battered and forlorn Jennifer had this dynamic creature inside her that could pop out when she was too depressed to function. I probed her eyes, looking for a trace of Jennifer in the glint of Margaret's pupils. Nothing. Jennifer was absolutely nowhere to be found. It was the body Jennifer used, but Jennifer wasn't there. I shook my head and smiled.

"What're you smiling about?" she asked.

"You."

"You think I'm funny?"

"No. Actually, I think you're fantastic."

"Sure you do."

"I really do."

"I know. Like somebody in a zoo, right?"

"No. Like some fascinating work of art."

"Sure." She yawned. "Are we finished yet?"

Occurred to me about midway during this session that Margaret (and the other personalities) is Jennifer's unconscious. She has a walking unconscious. Most people have unconscious thoughts and fantasies. Asking Margaret about Jennifer's feelings is like talking directly to Jennifer's unconscious. So Jennifer's afraid of me and wants to please me. The typical hysterical mode of relating to men. Denial of aggression; projection of that aggression onto the external object: men.

Wonder when Jennifer will return? Worried about her. Also wondering about myself—why has she moved me so much? I've traced it to a combination of factors. Certainly the multiple personalities are important—but I was entranced before that. Is it because nature has generously endowed Jennifer with such an abundance of intelligence, talent, grace, charm, and beauty? I've treated other intelligent, talented, and beautiful women and not been so touched. Is it that she had such a severely traumatic childhood? I've worked with other severely traumatized patients and not been so empathetic. Is it her childlike seductiveness? Her vulnerability? Her determination? Her potential to succeed despite her difficulties? Perhaps all of the above. There are certain people who make you care about them, who stand above the crowd. They're the people who are up-front with their feelings, who don't defend in the usual ways. Not that Jennifer always verbalizes her feelings, but they're out for all to see—her vulnerability, rage, and fear; her girlish seductiveness her intense determination; and, perhaps most important, her aversion to feeling sorry for herself. She has pride and dignity, in spite of everything. At times she hates herself, but at times she can love herself in a healthy, realistic way.

Spoke to my former supervisor on the phone. He informed me that he had never had a multiple in his thirty years of practice. Few have. Until recently they were considered rare. Only eight had been reported in the literature by 1970. Now, after more research, they're a bit more common, probably due to more accurate diagnoses. Feel a little afraid I might be in over my head. I tell myself I'll make up for my lack of experience with an abundance of empathy, therapeutic talent and beginner's zeal. We'll see.

ACH DAY a new surprise. Today Mildred—confident, gentle, and demure. Not a trace of Jennifer in her, nor of Margaret. The expressions that came on her face were completely her own, as was the soft, articulate voice with a midwestern accent. Wore a cotton summer dress. Sat ladylike, with legs together. Hair pulled back from her temples with blue clips that matched her eyes, hanging free below the temples, dropping around her shoulders. Pinkish shade of lipstick. Light brown eyeliner.

"Which one are you?" I asked.

She blinked gently, smiling at me as though she knew things I could never know, but it was all right, she accepted my limitations. "I'm Mildred," she said softly.

"You're the writer?"

"Yes. Sort of."

"What are you writing?"

"At the moment I'm working on two books. One is an autobiography of Henrietta Ross. The other is a book on the psychobiology of dance."

"The psychobiology of dance. That's interesting." I smiled at her and she smiled back. It was a completely unassuming yet at the same time completely assuming smile. It said nothing. It said everything that's ever been said about man and woman. Or so it seemed. Unlike Jennifer, who looked apologetically or fearfully at me, or Margaret, who glared, Mildred smiled in an open, responsive way, neither frightened of nor angry at me. Felt an immediate attraction to her. "So, you're interested in psychology?"

"Very much so. Actually, at the moment I'm particularly interested in suicide. Which is one of the reasons I came in today." She seemed like one of the sanest women I have ever met. "I was wondering if you had any suggestions about how to handle Jennifer's suicidal impulses."

"The most important thing is that she needs to talk about the things that are troubling her."

"How would that help her?"

"She's holding on to a lot of feelings—about her mother, her father, for example. The first thing she needs to do is let go of these feelings, which are overwhelming her. She has a lot of anger inside her, and she's taking it out on herself."

"Yes, I've heard that depression is anger turned inward. But the thing is, Jennifer's not really angry at her parents right now. She's feeling sad about Henrietta."

"Then she needs to come in and talk about Henrietta."

"I see."

I smiled. She smiled. I looked away. Her direct, open gaze seemed charged with innuendo. I looked back, amazed. I could still recognize Jennifer's body in front of me, but it was as though an alien force had taken it over— a friendly, advanced, beautiful alien. This new creature was contented with herself, wholesome and undefensive. Did not ever seem to have been hurt in her life. Where was Jennifer's depression? Margaret's rage? Not a trace in her manner or expression. Amazing.

As I gazed at her, something she had said stuck in my mind. "You said *'her'* parents." I looked at her. "Aren't they *your* parents, too?"

"No, they aren't," she replied in her soft-spoken way.

"Well, if you're one of Jennifer's personalities, then wouldn't her mother be your mother?"

"Heaven forbid!" She laughed softly. "I'm not one of Jennifer's personalities. We're all separate people."

"In the same body?"

"Yes."

"Then what do you consider Jennifer? A friend?"

"Yes. A close friend."

"How about the others? The other separate people? Does Margaret consider Jennifer's parents to be her parents?"

"Yes. She, Jess, Jenny and Tom are all brothers and sisters."

"That's five. There's one other person, right?"

"Mary. She's another close friend."

She folded her hands, smiling congenially. I wondered what to say next. She seemed so incredibly healthy, yet obviously out of touch with reality. Had a feeling I could reach her if I just found the right method. Thought of the book, *The Three Christs of Ypsilanti*, about how three schizophrenics who had the same Christ delusion were put in the same room and got well. By being confronted with the mirror image of themselves, they saw the delusion. I decided to mirror Mildred.

"You know, *I'm* a multiple personality," I said.

"Are you?" She smiled.

"Really. See that painting up there? Philip did it."

"Philip?" She glanced at the painting. "It's quite good, actually. I like it."

"Yes, Philip's quite talented. He's still a child. Only seven years old." I looked at her. "You don't believe me, do you?"

"Sure I do."

"And I have other personalities. I have an angry, moody personality and an outgoing personality. I even have a female personality."

"Oh, really. What's her name?"

I had to think for a minute. "Jazz. Her name's Jazz."

"That's an interesting name. What personality are you now?"

"Now? I'm the therapist personality." She nodded, pretending to go along with me. "Really, I'm a multiple personality. Only I'm a multiple and I *know* it. You still don't know you're one."

"I'm not a multiple personality," she said, gently.

"You're not. All right, if you say so." That tack hadn't worked, try another. "Let me ask you something. When were you born?"

"In 1972."

"In that case you'd be seven years old."

"No." She smiled and shook her head. "I'm twenty-nine—the same age as Jennifer."

"How could that be?"

"It just is."

"Then you were born at the age of twenty-two."

"Yes."

"Who are your parents?"

"I don't have any."

"You were born without parents?"

"Yes."

"You just appeared suddenly out of nowhere as a twenty-two-year-old woman?"

"Yes."

"No parents at all."

"Sort of."

"What are you smiling about? Doesn't this sound at all strange to you?"

"No."

"You don't think, seriously, that you're part of Jennifer—one of her personalities?"

"No. We're two separate people."

"But you're not separate. You have the same body."

"But we're still separate people."

I shook my head. "I give up."

She laughed in her gentle, pleasant way and smiled sympathetically.

"You're incredible," I said.

"Thank you."

"You seem so levelheaded, though."

"I am levelheaded."

"But not levelheaded enough to grasp the reality that you and Jennifer are one." I couldn't resist one last attempt.

"We're not one," she gently replied. "If we were, I would tell you we were." She smiled again. "It just isn't so."

I gave up trying to raise her consciousness and began instead to simply find out more about her. At one point I asked her about her name. Wanted to know if she was named after somebody.

"I made it up," she said.

"Does it have some symbolic meaning?"

"Yes. Guess what it means?"

"Mildred? Is it a kind of flower?"

"No. I'll give you a clue. Say it in two syllables."

"Mil. Dred."

"Try it again." She smiled.

"Mild. Red."

"I'm the *mild* red, you see?" She smiled, pulled a few strands of her orange hair out, and pointed at it. "You see?"

TWO WEEKS, no Jennifer. I'd begun to worry, thinking her disappearance meant trouble. Inquired about her to both Margaret and Mildred. Was she about to cut herself? Was she going to attempt suicide? They both said she wasn't. Perhaps my repeated inquiries brought her back. Today she appeared for her afternoon session.

"I don't remember anything at all," she said, confusion and sadness clouding her features. "I woke up this morning and had to call the operator to ask her what day it was. . . . It's really embarrassing to have to ask somebody what day it is. . . ." She was sitting on the floor again, in jeans, her back against the wall, legs folded, rubbing the palms of her hands against her thighs in a slow, mechanical motion, as though to stir up heat. Her eyes had the muted, gray Thorazine look. "I had no memory of the last two weeks," she said. "And then I saw the note on the telephone table."

"What note? What did it say?"

"It said, 'Therapy appointment today, 4:00 P.M.' "

"You didn't write the note?"

"No." She shook her head morosely.

"How do you know?"

"It wasn't my handwriting."

"Then you're saying it was written by one of your other personalities?"

"I don't know. . . . I don't know who wrote it. I find notes and things in other people's handwriting, and sometimes I hear their voices in my head." She looked out the window, in a daze. "Once, a few years ago, I decided to keep a diary. It started out being my diary . . . but then I discovered other people had written in it. They all seemed to know each other. . . . It was . . . embarrassing. . . ."

"What happened to the diary?"

"I destroyed it. . . ."

"Why?"

"I didn't want anybody to read it. . . . They might think I was . . . you know . . ." Her voice trailed off.

She looked down at her hands as they rubbed against her thighs. I looked at her hands, too. Attractive hands, long and pink with freckles. Moving gracefully back and forth, back and forth, in a hypnotic motion. Felt her deep sadness, saw how it weighed down her every cell. How could this deep sadness suddenly disappear from her when she changed to Mildred? Where did it *go*? If it became repressed, wouldn't it still lodge somewhere in her physical being? Seems it's accomplished through a form of hypnosis. She, in effect, hypnotizes herself to be a certain way and it happens. But where does the sadness go?

Tried to think of something to say, something about her blackout, the diary, Margaret and Mildred, the pain she was feeling and the pain they didn't feel. Somehow, even though I knew she wouldn't be able to hear it, I wanted to tell her about her personalities. I looked at her, waiting. She kept rubbing her thighs, but now with a new variation, pausing every now and then to grab her thighs with her thumb and fingers and squeeze them. From the desk the fan made a cyclical whirr as it rotated from left to right, in counterpoint to her movements.

"Jennifer, who do you think wrote those other parts of your diary?"

"I don't know."

"Did it ever occur to you that those other parts were written by other parts of yourself?"

"No. Not really."

"You've heard about multiple personalities, haven't you?"

"I'm not one of them!" There was a gush of desperation and anger in her voice.

"Are you sure?"

"I'm sure . . . !"

"Then how do you explain the notes? The diary? The voices in your head?"

"I don't know. . . ." The hands on her thighs were moving faster.

"Do you *want* to know?"

She didn't answer. Turned her head away from me. Gazed out the window. Rubbing her thighs, squeezing them, caressing them. Gazing with confused eyes, as though she wanted to form another personality at that moment, one that might fly to the trees, the wind, the sky.

As I write this I still feel her sadness and fear inside me. Stayed with me all afternoon as I worked with other patients. I feel her feeling of doom today more than ever, and I find myself thinking maybe she's right. Maybe I'm fooling her into believing she could have anything but a miserable existence. Maybe she sees the world accurately and the rest of us are deluded into thinking that existence has some redeeming value. Maybe she sees the cruelty the rest of us ignore. (Before he died, Freud was asked if he regretted leaving the world, and he replied that he rather looked forward to it, having spent a lifetime studying and being subjected to mankind's infinite stupidity and cruelty.)

It's staggering to realize that a parent could do that to a three-year-old child, and to witness the results of that childhood cruelty. I've often brooded about my own childhood, but it was nothing like hers. *Her* past makes mine look benign.

However, her past and mine have become commingled now, and I sit feeling paralyzed. I can scarcely lift this pen.

FOR SEVERAL sessions I've been pressing Jennifer to do bioenergetics. She's deluged with feelings that are toxic to her, and bioenergetics would seem to offer a way to release these feelings before she takes them out on herself. She's not only carrying all the hurt and rage from her childhood, but also the anxiety of her imminent separation from Henrietta Ross. She's at the breaking point. Full of humiliations and hostilities that she was never able to express to anybody, never able to get any soothing for, brimming to the surface, coming out in her depression, her suicidal impulses, her self-mutilation, and her dissociation into other personalities.

Why does she do it? Each attempt at suicide, each act of self-mutilation, is an act of revenge and an act of abandonment, directed toward those she feels injured and abandoned by. Overwhelmed with loneliness and despair, she takes out her revenge on the object—herself—which has been abused and abandoned by her mother, father, and others. "You want to abuse me? Fine, I'll abuse myself even worse, then you'll be sorry." But they never are.

On top of everything else, she suffered another separation this week—she and her friend Bonnie broke up after an argument on the telephone. This event put her in touch with all the other separations: from Henrietta, from her mother (her mother's sexual violence being a kind of separation, a loss of motherly protection and love), from several therapists, and from the men in her life. Having been pressed into service as a rescuer of her mother, particularly in her adolescent years, when she would often put her mother to bed in a drunken stupor and take care of her younger children, Jennifer had a habit of playing the rescuer and helper of alcoholic men. Barry was one such man. She literally picked him out of the gutter and helped to rehabilitate him, supporting him while he finished graduate school, after which he dumped her for another woman. Because of her fear of being abandoned she seems always to induce people into abandoning her.

This evening, after several prior attempts, she finally agreed to try the kicking and screaming exercise. She came in looking pale, forlorn, anxious, talking in starts and stops about Henrietta, Bonnie, and a training group she was attending.

"I feel all alone . . . my support system is falling apart," she said. "I'm losing Henrietta . . . I've lost Bonnie . . . and I'm probably going to have to give up my dance group." She sat on the floor, sighing, squeezing her thighs, her eyes slightly moist and looking dazed.

"What happened to Bonnie?"

"I don't know. . . . She called me this weekend and said she was angry at me for telling her she needed therapy. I don't remember saying that . . . I guess it must have happened while I was blacked out. Then she said she didn't want to have anything more to do with me because she felt I was too destructive. . . ." She whimpered. "And last night I felt alienated from everybody in my dance group . . ."

"What dance group?"

"I go to a dance-therapy group on Wednesday nights. It's sort of a training group. . . . I'm supposed to be learning to be a dance therapist. But I feel as if it's hopeless, as if I'm behind everybody else in the group . . . out of it. . . ."

"Is that why you're going to give it up?"

"That and because I can't afford it."

She began to tremble. Hugged herself. Gazed downward. Frantic. "I think the Thorazine is beginning to lose its effect." Her pallor backed her up.

"You're shaking," I told her.

"Am I?" She looked at me, surprised.

"What're you feeling?"

"I'm not sure . . . like I'm falling apart. . . ." Her eyes were unable to focus on anything. "I feel out of it. For one thing I guess I'm pretty stoned. No, I don't guess, I *know* I'm pretty stoned. I took two Thorazine capsules this morning, then two drinks of scotch, and then smoked a joint. . . ." She sighed and trembled.

"Did you by any chance visit your parents this weekend?"

"Yes, I did. I had to. My mother's typing up the tapes . . . the tapes of my interviews with Henrietta. She's transcribing them for me."

"Why did you ask *her* to do it?"

"Because she needed the money. . . ."

"Still trying to rescue your mother? How about rescuing yourself?" The words rushed out of me before I could think. Knew it was wrong as soon as I said them. She'd induced me to get angry at her as she did with almost everybody. Inducing people to be mean to her justified her martyrdom, was part of her masochistic pattern. I needed to break the pattern, not reinforce it. "If she's transcribing the tapes, will that mean you'll be seeing a lot of her?" I asked more calmly.

"Yes. Anyway, I'll be seeing her again this weekend. I have to go to my brother's wedding."

"It seems to upset you every time you see your mother."

"I know."

"Then why do you see her?"

"I have to see her. She's my mother. Anyway, she's changing. She's getting . . . better. . . ."

"Did she say something to upset you this weekend?"

"It was nothing really. . . . I told her I'd been in the

hospital again and she got angry at me. . . . She thinks I'm weak . . . doesn't believe in doctors or hospitals. . . ." She sighed, pinched her thighs. "When I was a kid she'd never take me to a dentist. . . . I shouldn't have told her . . . it's my own fault, I should have known. . . ."

"She never took you to a dentist? What if you had a toothache?"

"She'd pull it out with a pair of pliers if you complained to her about it. . . . After a while I just stopped complaining and kept it to myself. All my front teeth are false. . . ."

Myself now full of fury. Wanting to get angry at her like her mother had, wanting to lecture her, shout at her. Wanting to order her to stop seeing her mother. Kept telling myself that my job is to help the patient understand, not to run her life. But she was a borderline, in crisis. Falling apart. And she kept going back to the source of her misery, like a moth flying around a lightbulb. Amazing. The more a child is abused, the more she tends to cling to her abuser. What to do?

"Jennifer, you're all pent-up. We need to take the edge off. I'm going to show you an exercise. I'd like you to lie down on the couch like this." I lay on the couch and demonstrated the kicking, hitting, and screaming exercise. I stood up and looked at her. She was trembling, her head nodding. "Jennifer, did you see what I just did?"

". . . Yes. . . ." She was gazing away, her eyes glazed, shuddering with each breath.

"You're trembling. Your body's straining to hold everything in. Jennifer? Are you listening? Lie down on the couch."

"I . . ."

"Just lie down."

"It won't do any good."

"How do you know?"

"Why bother? It's no use. . . ."

She lay stiffly on the couch, staring up at the ceiling, arms pressed against her sides, legs stuck straight out, toes up. I had her take off her shoes.

"Now, start kicking. Put your knees up. Kick down on the couch."

"It's no use, I'm hopeless."

"Kick down. Stamp your feet."

She kicked feebly, gazing up at the ceiling. ". . . I can't. . . ."

"Yes, you can. Bang your fists into the couch."

"I . . ." She was swallowing back tears, making whimpering sounds. She was almost there, it wouldn't take much.

"Hit with your arms," I said, standing over her.

"It's . . ." Her arms and legs were moving in slow motion, barely touching the cushion. ". . . hopeless."

"Jennifer!"

"I'm no good. I'm sorry. I'm no good. . . ." She stopped moving.

"All right. You're hopeless. Have it your way." I sat back on the chair with my arms folded. I thought that by joining her resistance I'd be able to give her that push she needed. It didn't work. She kept holding it in, whimpering, swallowing. "I'm sorry. . . ." she kept saying. "I'm sorry. . . ."

But at least it was a start.

AT JENNIFER'S APARTMENT

I'VE JUST come from Jennifer's place. She called me a few hours after she left my office. Had taken all the sleeping tablets out of the bottle and placed them on the night table. Felt overwhelmed.

"Can you come in?" I asked.

". . . don't know. . . . I feel paralyzed . . . afraid to move. . . ."

"Try to make it in."

I had another patient to see, then phoned her back. She was still at home. Her voice hardly audible on the phone. I decided I had to make a house call.

She lived in a tenement building on the Upper East Side, a two-floor walk-up, rent-controlled. Apartment tastefully furnished with an old Persian rug, some antiques, prints of Impressionistic art. She let me in looking apologetic, frightened, meek. Eyes bulging. Walking stiffly. Trembling. I took the mattress from her bed and placed it on the floor.

"All right, Jennifer. You know what to do. Lie on your back like you did this afternoon. I think you're ready now."

"I'm sorry," she whispered. "I'm sorry to be such a bother."

"It's okay. Lie down. That's right. Now lift up your knees. Stamp your feet. Hit with your fists. Make a noise."

"I'm sorry . . . I'm really sorry. . . ."

"There's nothing to be sorry about."

"I . . . I . . ."

"Stamp harder."

"I . . ." She shook her head, trembling spastically.

She began to sob and cry from her belly. Turned away from me, facing the wall. Hugging herself. Tensing up her back. Gasping for breath. Trying with all her might not to cry. Going against a lifetime of conditioning not to cry. Whenever she'd cried as a child, her mother would tell her she was stupid, weak, a crybaby. Now, crying feelings of stupidity, powerlessness, abandonment. "I don't want to feel this way! . . ." She whimpered. "I don't . . . I don't. . . ."

"Let it out."

"I . . ."

"Jennifer!"

Finally it came. I sighed with relief, watching her cry. It was one of the most satisfying experiences I've ever had. Her tears were a lament for all the secret sins of the forefathers and foremothers. Crying from her belly, deeply, angrily. Stopping to lift her head, as if coming up from drowning, breathing quickly, desperately, dropping her face down on the couch, going at it again. It was beautiful.

"That's right," I said. "That's right."

"I'm no good," she kept repeating. "I'm no good. . . . I don't want to feel it." These first cries were judgmental cries, containing the incorporated harping voice of her mother. Her mother had told her over and over again that she was no good. She had taken part in evil acts with her mother. It was her fault. She was evil. Crying did no good. She couldn't cry the evil out. She was no good. Don't even try. So her mother had told her.

"I don't want to feel this way. . . ." she kept repeating.

But she could no longer not feel that way. The impasse had been broken. She cried for an hour. I sat behind her, silently watching over her, flooded with my own memories, holding back my own tears.

THE DAM has burst. She's been crying for the last three sessions. It's become routine. She comes in, lies on the couch, and assumes the kicking, hitting, and screaming posture. I no longer have to say anything. Usually she begins by screaming, "No, no, no," until she starts to cry. Takes only a few minutes before she's sobbing away. Cries in a characteristic way, flopping over onto her belly, burying her face into the cushion, sobbing for a few minutes, blurting, "I'm no good," stopping to raise her head and gasp for air, then crying some more. Sometimes when she says "I'm no good" she bangs her forehead against the pillow, as though wanting to injure herself. Sometimes she stops to tell me about a new memory.

Can't stop thinking about the dream she recalled a few sessions ago. She was about seven, had run away from home to a Catholic church a few blocks from her house. Told the nuns about how her mother and father were abusing her. Said she was scared her mother was going to kill her. Then related to them the recurring dream she was having, about a big red train with a big engine going very fast down a long, dark tunnel. In the dream there was a wall at the end of the tunnel, and her mother was tied against the wall, and the train smashed into her mother and the wall, crushing her against it. After telling the dream, she begged the nuns to let her stay with them. They said, "Don't talk about your mother and father that way" and "What a naughty dream." Took her home, informed her parents she had told on them. When the nuns left, her father beat her up in front of the whole family, cursed her, and called her a traitor. From then on she was the outcast of the family.

"My father had a violent temper," she said after having this memory. "There were lots of times I'd try to run away from him and fall on the floor and he'd kick me while I was on the floor. I'd be in a ball on the floor, trying to protect myself, and he'd kick me in the back. I remember . . . he used to come home at two or three in the morning and if he found a dish that hadn't been washed or a speck of dirt someplace he'd yank me out of bed and whip me with his belt. I used to be petrified at night, waiting for him to come home. I always slept on my back so I'd be ready. I still do. And if my mother had been drinking, he'd blame me for that, too. I was supposed to keep a watch over her. If he found a bottle of whisky around, he'd yank me out of bed and beat me, and then he'd beat up my mother and rape her. . . ." Her crying jags have been punctuated by many such memories.

She came to her session today upset once again about her father, after having gone home for her brother's wedding. It was a big, rural Pennsylvania wedding, and her whole family was there. When she came through the door, her head bowed, the anxious, apologetic expression on her face, I knew something had happened. Noticed a new scab on her arm. Asked why she had cut herself.

". . . Because I'm no good. . . ."

"What happened at the wedding?"

"I don't remember. . . ." She sat on the couch, hugging herself, shaking her head slowly.

"You had another blackout?"

"Yes. . . . I don't remember anything about the wedding. I remember taking the bus there and then riding the bus back with my older sister and her boyfriend Max. And feeling like they were angry at me and snubbing me. . . ." She sighed and shrugged. "And then . . . on Sunday morning my father called and accused me of acting like a whore at the wedding, and my sister called and said I'd been flirting with her boyfriend. . . ."

"Well, maybe Jess came out and did something. I understand you have a personality named Jess who acts that way."

"I don't know . . ." She sighed, trembled, and swallowed back tears, rubbing the newest cut mark on her forearm. "I don't understand why I feel so . . . so overwhelmed. . . ."

"A lot of feelings are coming to the surface. All the pent-up hurt you've been carrying around since childhood."

"Why did I cut myself?"

"It seems as though everybody's angry at you. Everybody thinks you're no good. Maybe you needed to punish yourself to get their sympathy, to atone for your sins."

"I can't stand feeling this way. . . ."

"Jennifer, let's do some more kicking and hitting."

"I'm scared. . . ."

She reluctantly began kicking and hitting. Arms and legs moving as though through mud. Before long, she was crying full out. This time it went somewhat differently. Started out blaming herself as usual, at one point moaning, "Do me a favor . . . kill me. Please, please kill me. I'm no good. I'm no good. . . ." When she turned to lie on her belly, banging her forehead into the couch, the crying gradually changed. It was angry, indignant. "I'm not a bad person, I'm good, it's not fair." Now she hammered the cushions with her fists. She had transformed into another personality during the crying—had become Jenny.

She was still crying at the end of the session. Since it was the last one of the day, I stuck with her. But I needed a break, having worked all day, so I told her I had to make a telephone call and would be right back. I went out and walked around the block, called the friend I was to meet to cancel our engagement, and walked some more. Filled with a mixture of emotions: excitement, sadness, sympathy, love, and above all, awe. That she could throw herself into these painful feelings and cry them out in front of me was deeply moving. We were almost perfectly in tune with one another. There was a trust there that was like no other trust I had ever felt—like the trust between a mother and infant.

I wondered, as I walked around the block a second time, how she could still have this capacity to trust somebody completely after what she had gone through. She had not been able to trust her mother, father, or siblings. There must have been somebody in her childhood with whom she had established a trusting relationship, but so far she had not mentioned anybody.

After about fifteen minutes I returned to the office. Found her sitting up on the couch. Legs were tucked under her. Holding a stuffed doll I had bought in Japan and kept on my bookshelf. Sucking fiercely at her thumb. There was a radiant glow in her eyes—the kind of glow children have after a good cry. I surmised she had turned into Jenny, glad to meet another personality. It was uncanny how childlike her posture and facial expressions were. Sat down on the couch beside her, marveling at her for a moment. She didn't look at me.

"I see you found the doll," I said.

Didn't answer. Sat the doll on her lap, adjusted its clothing, ignoring me. Rocked the doll in her arms. "I had a doll once," she said at last, still not looking at me. "My mother wouldn't let me play with her."

"How come?"

"My aunt sent it to me from Ireland. It was a beautiful doll. It was the most beautiful doll you ever saw. It was made of—" She looked at me. "I forget what it's called." She smiled shyly.

"Porcelain?"

"That's right. It was porcelain. It was so shiny and pretty."

"Why wouldn't your mother let you play with it?"

"She said it was too nice for me to play with. She said I wouldn't know how to play with such a nice doll. She put it away in a drawer and wouldn't let me play with it. But sometimes, when she wasn't there, I'd take it out and play with it. I'd talk to it and tell it that someday I'd rescue it and we'd run away together. Then when we moved to a new house the doll got lost. My mother said she didn't know what happened to it." She cradled the doll in her arms, brushed its hair back. "This is a nice doll, too. I like dolls more than people. People are mean."

"All people?"

"No, not all of them. Just most of them."

She walked the doll up and down on her legs.

"Are you Jenny?"

She nodded and smiled. A disarmingly bright and peaceful smile. Blue eyes sparkling. Giggled as she unfastened the doll's dress and tossed it aside. "This doll doesn't have any nipples." Then she grew serious again, laying the doll on her lap, caressing it.

"Jenny, how old are you?"

She held up five fingers of one hand, the index finger of the other.

"I see. May I ask you something else?"

"This doll needs some new clothes." She put the doll's dress back on, carefully, devotedly.

"Jenny, may I ask you something else?"

"What?"

"Was Jennifer around when your mother wouldn't let you play with the doll?" I was interested in finding out how and when she had first appeared. My hunch was that she represented Jennifer's first dissociation. "Do you know Jennifer?"

"I don't know what you mean."

"Well, who was born first, you or Jennifer?"

"Jennifer."

"So she was already there when you came?"

"Mm-hmm."

"How old was Jennifer when you came?"

She held up three fingers. "Three."

"Did something happen to her when she was three, at the time when you came?"

"You ask a lot of questions." She held the doll on her lap, looking at it with satisfaction. "My mother used to get mad at me for asking a lot of questions."

"Are you getting mad at *me* for asking a lot of questions?"

"No." She stood the doll on top of her knee. "Does this doll have a name?"

"Not yet. Would you like to name her?"

"I can't name her." She frowned at me, as though I were ridiculous.

"Why?"

"Because she's not my doll."

"All right. I'll name her. How about if we call it Dolly."

"Dolly! That's a silly name."

"Are you going to answer my question?" She paid no attention to me. "Jenny? Did something happen to Jennifer right before you came?"

"I'm not going to tell you."

"Why?"

"Because."

"Because isn't a reason."

"It's not nice, what she did."

"What who did?"

"I can't tell you."

She wouldn't look at me. I sat next to her, quite aware of her as a little girl, a special little girl with a very dynamic presence, and also aware that Jennifer was somewhere inside her, unconscious. She was dancing the doll along the arm of the couch. "You can't tell me what your mother did?"

"I'm not supposed to tell anybody."

"Is that when you first came? When Jennifer's mother first made Jennifer sleep with her?"

She nodded the head of the doll. "I used to pretend I was on a beach when she was doing that. She didn't know I was there. She thought it was still Jennifer. You won't tell her I told you, will you?" She looked at me.

"No. It's our secret."

"You ought to let other people play with your doll. I think she wants to be played with."

"Well, from now on whenever you're here you can play with her."

"Okay."

"Jenny, I have to go now. Would you like me to walk you home?" I was concerned about a six-year-old walking home, though later I realized I shouldn't have been. She would have changed into another personality while walking home. "I'm going that way anyway."

"Okay."

I locked up the office and the two of us headed down Fifth Avenue together. We were both silent for a while. She walked gaily beside me, the innocent glow in her eyes, which shone with the reflection of the street lamps. Walking in long strides, looking down at the sidewalk as she did so. Thought she was trying to keep up with me.

"You walk funny," I said.

"Step on a crack, break your mother's back," she said.

She was carefully stepping over the cracks in the sidewalk.

"You don't want to break your mother's back?"

"That's not nice."

"I suppose not."

We walked on for another block or two in silence.

"I don't think all grown-ups are mean," she said. "I think you're nice."

"Thank you. I think you're nice too."

"Do you think I'm smart?"

"Very smart."

"My mother doesn't think I'm smart."

"Do you think you're smart?"

"Yes." She smiled modestly. "I think I'm very smart."

"That's all that matters."

"Are you going to get Dolly a new dress?"

"Sure. What kind of dress should I buy her?"

"Pink and yellow."

"All right."

"Pink with yellow polka dots."

"Sounds good."

"And a hat. She needs a hat, a straw hat, for when she walks out in the sun."

I left her at the doorway of her building, then walked thirty blocks to my apartment. Occurred to me that Jenny had been in my office before—the session when "Jennifer" brought in "her" paintings. Thought about how Jenny had first emerged, on the heels of Jennifer's first traumatic sexual experience with her mother. The literature indicates that most multiples have been sexually or at least physically abused from an early age, usually before the age of three. Under extreme duress, before their egos have completely formed, they dissociate from themselves, form another self completely cut off from the pain of the trauma and from the self that was victimized and humiliated and made worthless by the trauma. This new personality, Jenny, seemed to have all the qualities that Jennifer lacked in dealing with her mother; while Jennifer could only meekly yield to her mother's domination and strive to win her approval, Jenny was a fighter who did not submit to her mother's tyranny and who had a mind of her own. Jenny represented a healthy adaptation to a psychotic situation.

As to why she remained stuck at the age of six, my theory is that the doll was a transitional object that was taken away from her. It represents a rite of passage from childhood to latency. By denying her the doll, her mother denied her this rite of passage. In a sense, she's still waiting for the doll to return. Or another doll—my doll—that will take its place and enable her to move on.

22

THE MORE I thought about what her parents did to her, the angrier I became at them. And when I thought about what they were still doing to her now, I felt angry at her for going back to them. She's in a precarious state. Each time she goes home she cuts herself and is on the verge of suicide. Had to take a stand. Crucial for her to break off her relations with them for the time being. Knew she wouldn't have the strength to do it on her own. Decided to confront her.

When she came in for her session, I waited only a minute or two until she settled into her place in the corner, then began with, "Jennifer, I have something to say to you, something very important, and I'd like you to hear me out." I told her that every interaction with her family set her off and put her in a suicidal mood. I went over each occasion she had visited home, and emphasized in the strongest possible terms how crucial it was for her to break with her family temporarily. I said there were several ways she could do it. The first was simply to not visit them or talk with them on the phone anymore. She didn't think she could do that, thought they'd want an explanation. In that case, I suggested, perhaps a simple letter might be best. It would be too difficult, I thought, for her to tell them in person or even on the phone. She agreed. I then proposed a letter, explaining that she could put it into her own words. "You could write something like, 'Dear Mom and Dad: My therapist has suggested that it would be best for me to temporarily curtail my social activities. I've been suicidal for a few months and, as you know, I was hospitalized for a week. He has recommended that for the time being I concentrate on my psychotherapy until I'm feeling more stable. I hope I can count on your cooperation in this matter.' "

She listened to the proposed letter with guarded interest. Sitting on the floor, sighing and rubbing her thigh. Her expression increasingly apprehensive. "I don't know," she said.

"What don't you know?"

"It's going to make my father very angry."

"But we're not saying it's his fault. The letter doesn't blame anybody."

"I know. But he'll take it that way just the same."

"What if he does?"

"I'm scared . . . scared of what he'll do. I'm scared he'll get violent. You don't know him."

"What are you afraid he'll do?"

"I'm afraid he'll come looking for me. I'm afraid he'll kill me . . . he'll hunt me down and kill me. . . ."

"I don't think he'll do anything like that. Deep down he realizes how much he and your mother upset you. Deep down they both know."

"No, they don't know." She shook her head. Her eyes were wide open and she was gazing at everything and nothing, her pupils darting to the left and to the right. "They don't think they've abused me, don't you see? . . . They think they've been good parents. . . . They go to church every Sunday. . . . They think they're good Christians and good parents. . . . My mother doesn't remember anything. . . . Oh, God, I'm scared."

"Jennifer, I feel very concerned about you," I said in a caring but firm tone. "It's a fact that you *are* suicidal right now, and it's an undeniable fact that your parents have a destructive effect on you. Jennifer, look at me. You have to write this letter. You have to do something. Do you hear me? If you can't write the letter, then you have to just stop going home. But I think the letter would make it easier. Then they'd understand and maybe leave you alone."

"What if they disown me?"

"They won't disown you. You're too important to them. You're their scapegoat. Scapegoats are very important to people."

"That's a pleasant thought."

"They won't disown you, believe me."

"But what if they do?"

"Think about it. What would you lose if they do?"

"They're all the family I've got. I'd feel all alone."

"We'll have to work on helping you establish a network of friends."

"But that's in the future. What about now?"

"For now you'll have to depend on me. As a matter of fact, I've decided to start seeing you more frequently. Don't worry about the money, you can pay me later."

"I'm scared. I'm scared to depend on you."

"Jennifer, it's not forever. It's only temporary. After you've worked through your suicidal feelings and are more stable you can see them again if you like."

"I hope we're doing the right thing. . . ."

"We are."

"I wish I were as sure as you." She hugged herself. "Why do I feel like crying?"

"Probably because despite everything you'd miss them."

She began to sob, then stopped herself. Sat in silence, gazing down, taking deep breaths.

"Go on, cry."

"No . . . I don't feel like crying today. . . ."

I didn't press her. She had done a lot of crying over the past several weeks. Needed some periods of rest.

We spoke some more about her parents and the letter, then during a lull in the conversation I called for Margaret. Between sessions I'd decided on a new intervention. Had Jennifer sit in the chair and close her eyes. Repeated to her several times that I wanted to speak to Margaret. Nothing happened at first. She just sat there with her head bowed. At last there was a movement. Jennifer looked up and she wasn't Jennifer anymore. Margaret's by now familiar scowl had taken over.

"What do you want?" she asked in a strident voice.

"I wanted to talk with you."

"What about?"

"For one thing, I wanted to ask you if there is any way you could let Jennifer be aware of when you've taken over her body."

"Why should I?"

"Because of the blackouts. When you take over, she goes unconscious."

"What's wrong with that?"

"It's bad for her. It makes her feel bad about herself and compounds her problems. Like with the Bonnie situation. You told Bonnie off, and then when Jennifer woke up she didn't understand why Bonnie was so angry at her. Things like this are always happening. It would be good for all of you if you were integrated."

"I'm not so sure of that. It's been working the way it is. We have a spirit of cooperation."

"If it's working so well, how come Jennifer's attempted suicide so many times and is on the verge of it again?"

"That's not because of us."

"Margaret, the blackouts have to stop."

She scowled at me. "We both want the same thing."

"We do?"

"We both want to be boss."

"I'm not trying to be the boss. I'm just trying to do what needs to be done," I said.

"You're being a boss. You're just like all men. They always want to be the boss."

"All right, I suppose you could say I'm being bossy.

But it's only a temporary thing, until Jennifer's out of trouble. Do you understand?"

She sat with her arms folded, scowling. "Are you finished with me now? Am I dismissed?"

"Actually, I wanted to ask you something else."

"Go on."

"Were you listening when I questioned Jenny about when she was born?"

"You want to know when I was born?"

"That's right."

"When Jennifer was thirteen."

"Did something happen at that time?"

"She was raped."

"Really? She never spoke about it. How did it happen?"

"What do you mean, how did it happen? She was raped."

"Where?"

"On the platform of the downtown subway, coming home one night from dance class. Three black teenaged punks raped her."

"You were born during the rape?"

"No. I came out afterwards, when her mother attacked her."

"What happened?"

"When she came home and told her mother what had happened, her mother went crazy. She was drunk as usual, and she went into a rage and took a whisky bottle and tried to jam it up her vagina. She pushed her against the wall and told her she was stupid and that it had happened because she was no good. She said if Jennifer ever let a man touch her like that again she'd kill her."

"That's when you first appeared?"

"Right."

"What did you do?"

"I yanked the bottle out of her hand and pushed her

against the other wall and shook her. I told her if *she* ever touched me again I'd kill *her*."

"That must have surprised her."

"She was in shock." Margaret smiled.

"Did she ever touch you—or Jennifer—again?"

"Nope."

"You must still have some feelings about that."

"So?"

"Would you like to talk about them?"

"No thanks." She smiled sarcastically. "I don't need therapy, and I don't need your sympathy."

After she left I thought about the situation. So Margaret had also emerged on the heels of a traumatic shock. This accords with the findings of other researchers. Morton Prince, in 1905, noted that Christine Beauchamp had first dissociated after a "nervous shock" when she was eighteen. Cornelia Wilbur, in her psychoanalysis of Sybil Dorsett, traced down the various traumas that had led to her multiple dissociations (eighteen in all). She came to believe that it was nurture, rather than nature, that caused the development of multiple personalities. Kluft, a psychiatrist, hypothesizes that a combination of nature (a predisposition to dissociation as a means of reacting to severe trauma) and nurture (severe trauma) both contribute. The questions that Prince, Wilbur, Kluft, and others had to consider were: Why does an individual form another personality? Is it solely because of the severe trauma? Then why don't all severely abused children develop multiple personalities? Do they form multiple personalities because they have been severely traumatized at such an early age? Again, not all children who have been severely traumatized at an early age develop multiple personalities. Kluft theorizes a predisposition in some children toward dissociation—toward the use of autohypnosis—as a means of defense.

As for nurture, if it is a traumatic shock that unleashes each new personality, are there other factors that also go into making that personality what it is? In Jenny's case, it seems that her personality traits were partly determined by the situation: she took over when Jennifer couldn't cope with an overwhelming shock, and she possessed the mental toughness and independence of mind to adapt to her mother's psychotic sadism. But this adaptation had to be done "in secret," because Jennifer herself had to repress any angry thoughts or impulses about her mother (lest her mother kill her for having them). Likewise, Margaret's emergence coincided with a need for Jennifer to react with counteraggression to her mother's aggression. Margaret embodies the aggression that Jennifer is not allowed to have. Due to her harsh superego, which introjects her parents' harsh judgments toward her ("I'm no good, I'm a slut," etc.), she must always strive to prove she is good, and to deny all negative thoughts and feelings.

Another question: is the process of identification involved in the formation of these and the other personalities? Wilbour thought so, and showed the multiple identifications of Sybil. Kluft found that identification played a part at times, but not always. Who does Jenny identify with? And Margaret?

Also interesting to note how closely Jennifer's family background fits the characterization of families of multiples in general, according to studies by Braun and Stern. They found that families of multiples invariably espouse rigid religious or mystical beliefs; present a united front to the community but are riddled with internal conflict; are isolated from the community and resistant to assistance; include at least one caretaker who is severely pathologic (an abuser), and another who is underadequate (an enabler); and subject the child to contradictory communications from the beginning.

I hope I got through to Jennifer about breaking off relations with her family. First things first. Get her stable, then worry about analyzing her.

SESSION

23

CAME IN distraught. Her parents had gotten the letter and her father had immediately called and blasted her. Wondered whether I was a quack. Asked her how she could do such a thing to her mother. Said he wasn't even going to show her the letter, it would be too upsetting to her. Yelled at her again about acting like a whore at the wedding.

"It's interesting that he wasn't at all concerned about the fact that you're suicidal," I pointed out.

"No, he didn't say anything about that," she replied. She was seated on the chair, not on the floor. "He thinks that's all . . . just some game I play. He doesn't believe there's anything really wrong with me. He says . . . I ought to read the Bible and . . . go to church. . . ."

"How do you feel now?"

"I have mixed feelings. In a way I feel relieved . . . but in another way I feel scared."

"That he might do something?"

"Yes."

"What might he do?"

"He might . . . destroy the tapes. My mother still has the tapes of Henrietta's autobiography. He might burn them up or something. . . ."

"You think he'd do something like that?"

"I wouldn't put it past him. I've never heard him so furious. The letter really got to him. He said he'd never heard of a therapist advising a patient not to see her parents. He said he was going to find out about you, find out if you're a quack or not. . . ."

"Let me worry about that."

"I also feel scared of being alone. They're the only parents I've got, and now . . ." She began to sob. Cried mournfully for a few minutes, then her crying grew louder, coming out in gushes. Shook her head and grimaced.

"What are you thinking about?" I asked.

"I was remembering something. I was remembering the time, right after I broke up with Barry, I went to this place . . . this place in New Jersey . . . a rifle range. I wanted to learn how to shoot a gun. I used to go there and practice shooting a rifle and I'd pretend I was shooting at my mother and my father. I'd see their faces in the target and . . . It's funny, I'd forgotten all about that. . . . I had it all planned, how I was going to go to my parents' house some evening when I knew they were there, barge in the door with the gun and shoot them down while they were watching television." There was a smile of surprised delight on her face. "I was really going to do it. In fact, I was so afraid I was going to do it I wrote them a letter warning them that I was going to do it, and practically begging them to have me locked up to protect themselves. . . ."

"How'd they react to the letter?"

"They didn't know what to make of it. Never answered it. I think maybe my father called me and said something about going to church. That's what he always says whenever I do something he doesn't approve of. Go to church. Pray."

"So what happened?"

"I ended up cutting myself. That's when I had my first nervous breakdown."

"You must have been pretty angry at your parents to want to kill them. You must have hated them."

"I did . . . and still do! I know I shouldn't, but I do, I really do hate them!"

She burst into sobs again. Crying angrily. Cried for the rest of the session, stopping to bring up more memories. I was glad that she, as Jennifer, had been able to acknowledge her hatred for her parents at last. This was a real milestone. But I was concerned about what her father would do now.

AT THE FAMILY HOUSE

KEPT WORRYING about the tapes. Wondered if there was really a chance her father would destroy them. Felt guilty about having suggested the letter to her family. If her father destroyed the tapes, it would be my fault. These tapes were important to Mildred. She had gone to great lengths to interview Henrietta, and the tapes were to be the basis of her biography. Very likely Jennifer was paranoid, but there was always a chance she was right.

Called her up on Saturday. A calm voice answered—Mildred. Asked her what she planned to do about the tapes. Said she didn't know. Did she think her father might destroy them? Said she thought there was a good possibility of it and was worried. Was there a way for her to go home unnoticed and retrieve them? Possibly, she thought, on Sunday morning when "Jennifer's parents" were at church. I suggested she do that, but she said she didn't have enough money for train fare since she wouldn't be getting her S.S.D. check for another week. I offered to lend her the money, but she refused. Said she'd be scared to go there alone anyway. Finally, after a long pause, I heard myself offering to drive her.

BALMY DAY near the end of June. Sun gleaming off the hood of my car as we drove along the New Jersey Turnpike toward Philadelphia. Radio crooning old favorites. Me, sitting stiffly behind the wheel, trying to maintain my therapeutic neutrality in this new, nonneutral setting, thinking about all the dates I'd had in cars, wondering if she was thinking the same thing, asking myself if I knew what I was doing. She, ensconced in her seat, also looking a bit stiff and worried, but pretty in her white blouse and floral print skirt, her legs folded under her, humming softly with the radio.

"Mildred," I said after a while, "may I ask you when you were born?" Decided to make use of the time by doing some therapy.

She laughed and mock-frowned. "I was wondering when you'd get around to asking me that."

"You were?"

"I was there when you asked Jenny and Margaret the same question. You have a theory, I take it, about the source of our personalities."

"Yes, I do." I explained the theory and noted that it wasn't my theory, that I was trying to corroborate other people's investigations and perhaps expand on them.

"I can tell you precisely when I first appeared. It was the day after Jennifer broke up with Barry. And, yes, she did feel overwhelmed by that experience. It was quite traumatic. You have to understand that Barry left her for a younger woman—this after she'd supported him for four years. It's the old story: he'd promised to marry her if she supported him while he went through graduate school. But after he graduated he no longer needed her. They were up in Maine, visiting friends, when he told her about the other woman. The next day she took the bus back to New York. That's when I first 'appeared'—as you put it."

"How old was Jennifer then?"

"Twenty-two."

"That seems to corroborate the theory. Let me ask you something else. Is there anybody you strongly identify with or admire?"

"I'm not sure about identifying with her, but I admire Henrietta tremendously."

"What do you admire about her?"

"I admire her mind. She's very quick, intuitive. And I

also admire her poise and confidence. She's always so calm. There doesn't seem to be anything she can't handle."

"Would you say you're like that?"

"I'd like to be."

Yes, it made sense that Jennifer would form a personality based on an identification with the woman she admired most.

"Do you know about the other personalities? Do you know when the others first made their appearance?"

"Only about Mary."

"What about her?"

"She appeared a year after me. I don't know anything about the ones who came before. She appeared when Jennifer had to sell all the antique furniture she and Barry had bought together. It was the day she had to move out of the apartment they had shared."

"Was that rough for her?"

"Terrible. She loved her antique furniture. She'd picked out each piece herself. And she loved their apartment. She had to give them up and move into this dinky roominghouse on Morningside Drive. At the edge of Harlem."

"That's when Mary came?"

"Yes. She came the day Jennifer moved into the roominghouse. Jennifer felt way down that day. Completely humiliated and unable to cope."

"What's Mary like?"

"She's very proper and proud. Aristocratic. Cultured. Likes museums and fine clothing and nice restaurants."

"That makes sense."

"What do you mean?"

"She appeared at a time when, as you say, Jennifer felt humiliated and impoverished. So it seems to me that she was created to provide what Jennifer needed to handle that particular situation. Her proud and aristocratic nature made up for Jennifer's fall from grace. She's a compensatory personality."

"A compensatory personality? I've never heard that term before. That's interesting. And what about me? Am I also a compensatory personality, according to your theory?" She flashed a wry smile.

"Yes. I would think so. You were created to compensate for Jennifer's feelings of inadequacy. When she was rejected by Barry for a younger woman, she must have felt quite inferior, lacking in the confidence to hold on to him. Didn't you tell me that Barry used to put down Jennifer's intelligence? Make fun of her writing?"

"All the time."

"You are the woman Barry wanted Jennifer to be. Poised, confident, calm, intelligent. Capable of handling any situation. Like Henrietta."

"You seem convinced I've identified with Henrietta."

"Yes."

"I'll have to give that some thought." She sat back, allowing her legs to drop from under her skirt. "You also seem to think Jennifer is the—how shall I put it—the trunk of the tree, and that all the rest of us are branches."

"Exactly. Jennifer's the original personality, the one who's been around since birth. All the rest of you came after her. It's a form of autosuggestion. Jennifer hypnotizes herself into becoming another personality, a personality that's threatening for her to assume consciously, because it embodies traits that are . . . well, the fancy term is ego-dystonic."

"What's *ego-dystonic?*"

"Threatening to the ego."

"Oh. Then you're saying I'm Jennifer hypnotized into being Mildred?"

"That's right."

"I don't buy it."

"Why not?"

"I'm not Jennifer. We're separate people."

"You're not separate people. You're separate personalities, but you're both aspects of one person."

"I don't think so."

"Are you sure?"

"Pretty sure."

She didn't seem as convinced as she had been. Felt her cracking a bit. No longer smiling at me as though I was being ridiculous to even suggest it. Which encouraged me to press on.

"Mildred, I've been thinking that it would be a good idea if you and Jennifer were integrated."

"I *know* you do."

"Were you around when I told Margaret to let Jennifer be aware of when she had taken over?"

"I was there."

"Well, I'd like you to do the same thing. I'd like you to let Jennifer know what's going on when you're out."

"Why?"

"Because she needs to be in control. Did you ever see or read the play by Pirandello, *Six Characters in Search of an Author*? Yes? Well, you're seven personalities in search of a coordinator. It's anarchy, you know what I mean? There's nobody to mediate between the seven different personalities."

"It's not that bad. We've been functioning pretty well most of the time. We're a team."

"Yes, but a team without a coach. And when a team without a coach loses a few games, it begins to fight within itself. Then it starts throwing games."

"That's quite a metaphor, but—"

"Mildred, somebody has to serve as the coordinator, don't you see? Somebody has to be the ego. And that somebody has to be Jennifer, since she's the core personality. She needs to be strong enough to mediate the various aspects of herself. She could use your wisdom and Margaret's strength. If she was aware of you it would increase her self-esteem and capability."

"But would I then pick up her low self-esteem and suicidal tendency?"

"That's a very good question." She had surprised me. Having had no previous experience with multiples, I didn't know what to answer. "It seems likely the two of you would reach a compromise."

"I'd be less contented and she'd be less suicidal?"

"Something like that."

"It doesn't sound too appealing. I'd like to cooperate with you. I believe in what you're doing for Jennifer. But . . . I don't know."

"The main thing is we've got to stop the blackouts. All I'm really suggesting is that you allow Jennifer to be aware of when you're out. Let her be conscious."

"I'm not sure I can do that."

"Can you tell if she's aware or not?"

"Sort of."

"Is she aware of what's happening right now?"

"I don't think so."

"Can you feel her inside of you?"

"Yes. I can feel her trembling."

"See if you can let her be aware. For the rest of the trip, see if you can let her see and hear what you're seeing and hearing. Okay? Otherwise she'll have a blackout today."

It took a little over two hours to reach the suburb of Philadelphia where Jennifer's parents lived. As we wound through the freeway over Philadelphia, our attention went to the practical matters of watching for traffic lights and getting off at the proper exits. Dawned on me that I felt guilty being with Mildred. Felt as if I were doing something behind Jennifer's back, was unfaithful to her by being so interested in Mildred. Constantly wondering what Jennifer was feeling. Assuming she knew what was happening on some level, that she was watching everything. Reacting. Taking notes. That was one of the reasons I wanted Mildred to let Jennifer be aware. Strange to feel guilty about being with a split-off part of Jennifer's self.

Then there were long periods of forgetting completely that Mildred was anybody else but Mildred. Thinking only that she was a person, an intelligent companion with whom I was discussing other people named Jennifer and Margaret and Mary. Then the thought would hit me again that Mildred was Jennifer being Mildred, and the feelings of guilt would return.

Also felt concerned, from a therapeutic point of view, that if I paid too much attention to Mildred, it would reinforce Mildred's sense of separateness while at the same time discouraging integration. She'd fight integration, want more of my attention. Also wondered whether Jennifer might see my attention to Mildred as a rejection of her and begin to feel even more inadequate and suicidal.

Reached the parents' house at about noon. A small, ordinary house covered with brown shingles, with a one-car garage to one side, a porch on which stood a couple of metal outdoor chairs, and a lawn of green carpet grass. It was on an ordinary street, one of those streets with houses all alike. Had an eerie feeling as I sat looking at this house where so much hidden cruelty had gone on. There was an aura of innocence about the house, with its all-American look. An aura that belied Jennifer's reports of the abuse and violence she had endured.

Mildred and I agreed it would be best if she went in by herself so as not to be more provocative than necessary. "If I don't come out in ten minutes, call the police," she joked. She was out in five, lugging a shopping bag containing the tapes, which she tossed into the back seat. Fortunately, no one was home.

"I'm shaking like a leaf," she said as we drove down the road.

"Are you sure it's you who's shaking, or Jennifer?"

"Perhaps a little of both. I'm not sure!" She smiled uncertainly.

We maneuvered our way back through the Philadelphia freeway and cruised out onto the turnpike toward New York in silence. The elation and relief at having retrieved the tapes had given way to a kind of exhaustion and, on my part, self-consciousness. I had once again become concerned that I had overstepped the boundaries of therapy. Felt vulnerable outside the sanctity of my office. Afraid I'd contaminated the transference. As I had no air conditioning, we drove with the windows slightly open, and a breeze wafted through the car. She seemed lost in thought. Her blue eyes gazing off, an expression of sadness I hadn't seen in Mildred's face before. Strands of hair flapping against the side of her face. Paying no attention to it.

"What are you thinking?" I asked.

She blinked, wiped her hair back, looked at me. "I was thinking about Jennifer."

"Oh?"

"I've never felt her inside me so strongly. I can really feel her feeling sad. It's amazing."

"I'm glad." I'd been using informal induction for some time and it was apparently starting to work. "Not glad that you're sad," I explained, "but glad that you're letting Jennifer in. What's Jennifer sad about?"

"She's sad about breaking off relations with her parents, and about Henrietta."

"How sad is she? Is she still suicidal?"

"Not really. More of a deep sadness. I feel her heaviness in my own chest."

"Is she aware of what's happening right now?"

"Yes, I think she is. I've been making a mental effort to talk to her all day, to try to allow her to participate in things."

"And it's working?"

"I think so. I've never felt like this before. That must mean something. I'm not sure I like it."

"What don't you like?"

"Experiencing her feelings. They're very heavy. And scary. I can feel her trembling inside me. And crying."

"Perhaps you could cry for her."

"I've never cried."

"Why not?"

"I like to maintain a positive outlook. Which is one of the reasons I'm not so sure I want to be integrated with Jennifer. I don't know if I want to feel this sadness all the time."

"But the sadness is there, whether you acknowledge it to yourself or not. She's a part of you. If she's depressed, she pulls all of the rest of you with her. If she commits suicide, the rest of you die too. You can't really separate yourself from her. That's an illusion."

"I'm beginning to think you may be right."

"Really?"

"Yes." She smiled ruefully.

"That's terrific."

"I guess so."

We drifted down the highway, each in our own thoughts. Then she asked if I'd mind if she found some better music on the radio and slid over on the seat, her arm grazing mine as she turned the dial. Settled on a station that was playing jazz tunes from the swing-band era. Stayed there in the middle of the seat inches away from me. I felt awkward about this and the romantic music. Also sad and lonely myself.

Thought about my ex-wife, about the way it had ended. After we'd separated I still longed for her, even though I knew it could never have worked. Then one night I saw her walking arm in arm with somebody else. Called her up the next day, yelping about how much I loved her, wanted her, needed her. "I'm sorry, it's over," she'd said. "I'm in love. We're talking about getting married." She added, "It's a shame, really. You could be lovable if you gave yourself half the chance." That had been a year ago.

Hadn't seen any other women since. Still missed her at times. Missed her again now. . . .

Mildred was sitting right next to me, humming. The music was soft and moody. Her hair had the scent of perfume. Could she sense my loneliness? I sat stiffly, my eyes riveted on the road. Getting a headache.

"You know, Mildred, I think . . . I think it would be better if you moved over a bit."

"I'm not sure what you're saying." She looked up with surprise. "Is there something wrong?"

"No, there's nothing wrong. It's just . . ."

"Yes?" She moved, but all the way to the window.

"I really care about you, Mildred."

"I really care about you, too."

"And I was worried about the tapes. That's why I offered to drive you today. It's just something I felt I had to do."

"I appreciate it."

"But I realize that in doing this I've changed the nature of our relationship. We're not in my office now, you see, and it's a different situation, a provocative situation. Do you understand?"

"Yes, I think I do."

"I mean, it's a normal part of any therapeutic relationship for a patient and therapist to have all kinds of feelings about one another. So far, we haven't talked about these things because we've been dealing with Jennifer's crisis. Do you know what I'm getting at?"

"Yes. Actually, I think I've probably been having the same kinds of thoughts myself. About this being a different situation, I mean."

"Then you understand?"

"Yes. I think so." She smiled in her earnest way.

When I let her off in front of her building we shook hands. Seemed we'd made an unspoken agreement. Felt better about things.

Now, as I write this, I'm not sure. The intense feelings

that were aroused during the trip, and suppressed, have now returned. Think I may be falling in love with her. Got to watch myself.

Excited by the possibility of her integration with Jennifer. Amazed that the process has apparently already begun.

"WHAT'S THE matter?" I asked.

"I don't know."

Jennifer sat down gingerly on the couch as though poised to make a quick run for the door. Her eyes sad and secretive, but her mouth stifling a shy smile. Unable to look me in the eyes. Held some sheets of notebook paper in her hands.

"What've you got there?"

A blush flashed and faded. "It's . . . a letter I found when I woke up this morning. I'm not sure what to make of it."

"What does it say?"

"It's about . . . what happened yesterday."

"Do you remember yesterday?"

"A little. . . ." A perplexed wrinkle between brows accented her smile.

"Wonderful. I suggested to Mildred that she let you be aware of things. What do you remember?"

She sighed, hugged her knees against herself, buried part of her face behind her knees. "I remember . . . I remember jazz music . . . and I remember driving down a highway . . . my parents' house. . . . It's all vague, as though I dreamed it."

"Better a dream than a complete blackout."

She held out the letter. "Do you want to read it?" She pulled it back. "I don't know if I want you to read it." Held it out again. "I guess you'd better. . . ." She looked down, embarrassed.

I took the letter in both my hands.

Dear Jennifer

Please do not be afraid. Everything will be all right. I deliberately logged everything that happened on Saturday in my memory. I think you can find access to it if you want. You will find some of next month's money gone. I needed it for tolls and gas. Don't worry about it. I will work as an office temp for a week if necessary.

Dr. S. drove me to the parents to pick up all the material for Henrietta's biography. We had a really good, fun time. We laughed a lot and talked a lot and listened to a great old jazz station. You would have enjoyed it. Dr. S. is a wonderful, loving, giving man. I have very strong feelings for him and am physically attracted to him.

I want you to know all this and not be scared, especially not of Dr. S. I am on your side. I want us to work together and be happy and productive. Please talk with Dr. S. about this and trust him. Also trust your feelings toward him; he is not out to hurt you. He cares about you and wants to help.

I love you and believe in you. You have the strength to get through all of the bad hurt feelings and memories. You can do anything you want to do. Believe in me and trust Dr. S. We are both on your side.

Much love,
Mildred

I have decided that we have to have a miraculous cure because I want to make love with this man.

Jess

Read the three-page, handwritten letter several times, chuckling at various points. Mildred's handwriting was large and feminine, with broad, round letters that leaned slightly backward. Jess—the "sexy" personality whom I had yet to meet—wrote in a scribbly, childlike way, with some letters leaning forward and some backward. When I finished reading I felt anxious. What had this trip wrought? "Why did you feel conflicted about showing me the letter?" I asked Jennifer.

Took her a long time to answer. Kept her eyes averted. Fidgeting on the couch. Hiding behind her knees, one blue eye blinking. "Do I have to take responsibility for what they say?"

"What do you mean?"

"I don't want to take responsibility for the . . . sexual feelings."

"Why not?"

"It scares me."

I explained to her, as I had with Mildred, that it was normal to have such feelings about one's therapist. It was good that they had now come up, I told her, because now we could talk about it. "In therapy we talk about everything," I said.

"It scares me to talk about that," she said.

"You'll get used to it."

"Anyway, I'd like to thank you for what you did. It was very generous of you to drive . . . Mildred . . . home to get the tapes."

"You—and Mildred—are quite welcome."

"I feel strange . . ." She whimpered, and I knew she was about to cry. "I don't know what's happening to me . . ."

"What do you think is happening?"

"It's . . . I can feel you really care . . . and that makes me sad. I don't know why . . ."

She lay down on the couch and cried in heaving sobs for the rest of the session.

JENNIFER CAME in again today with that shy, childlike, uncertain smile. Took a batch of papers out of her purse and dropped them on my desk. Sat on the couch, eyes averted.

"What's that?"

"Some poems I wrote."

"Do you want me to read them now?"

"If you like."

"When did you write these?"

"Last night. I couldn't sleep."

There were twelve poems she'd written quickly at the typewriter, about her fear of falling apart, her fear of depending on me, her fear of changes, her fear of trusting.

One stood out. It compared the flood of tears inside her to the lava in a volcano:

> Underneath the parched soil
> i lurked in darkness, numb;
> now unable to halt the billowing tide
> of formless matter deep inside
> i peer out of the void with trembling lids:
> the earth can no longer protect me,
> the sun will be my guide.

"It's beautiful," I said, amazed at her many talents. Wilbur, who has treated many multiples, claims to have never met one who had an IQ of less than 110. Most, like Jennifer, are multitalented. "I like it."

"Thanks."

"I see you've used the volcano metaphor again. How do you interpret the poem?"

"I think I've still got a lot of feelings that need to come out. I still feel overwhelmed. And . . . I guess it means I'm ready to trust you." She gave me a pointed look.

"That's nice."

But it wasn't so nice. Found myself feeling more and more anxious as we read through the rest of the poems. Couldn't figure out why. Only after she had left was I able to analyze it. I'm the Good Daddy she always longed for, the one she always hoped for from the darkest days of her infancy, who would rescue her from the Witch-Mommy and take her away with him on his white horse. Can I rescue her? The mere thought of it sends chills up my spine, spins a knot in my stomach. She's expecting me to be omniscient and omnipotent. She's expecting me to make her dreams come true. To love her, to have a relationship with her, to give her life meaning. That's a lot to expect from a therapist. What if I don't live up to her expectations? She's overwhelmed, and now I'm feeling overwhelmed too.

27

EVERY DAY she's depending on me more and more. Every day she's letting me know *how much* she's depending on me. She's quit her psychiatrist. Stopped taking the medication. I didn't ask her to. Would have felt more comfortable if she had kept seeing him, kept taking the medication, as a safeguard. But I didn't have a chance to add my input.

"It's finished," she said. Sitting on the floor again, anxiously rocking to and fro.

"What's finished?"

"I talked to my psychiatrist this morning."

"Oh. What happened?"

"I told him I didn't think he was helping me . . . that I didn't want to take the Thorazine anymore."

"And?"

"He said he didn't know if he wanted to take responsibility for me if I didn't take the Thorazine, and I told him that was okay because I was seeing you." A twinge shot through me as she said that. "I also told him about my work with you . . . about the bioenergetics."

"How did he react to that?"

"He didn't. He just repeated that if I didn't take the Thorazine he wouldn't take responsibility for me . . . so I told him I wanted to terminate. I brought up the incident when he fell asleep during the session. I told him I didn't think he was competent."

"You said that?"

"Yes . . . it was strange. I felt as if I were there but

not really there . . . .as if I were outside myself looking in. . . ."

"You must have been Margaret."

"I don't know. . . . It was strange. . . ."

"It means you're getting more integrated. Margaret's letting you be aware, too."

"I thought you'd like that." She smiled anxiously.

"So how do you feel, now that you've broken with your psychiatrist and gone off the drugs?"

"Scared. I hope I did the right thing."

"You can always go back to him if things don't work out."

"That's true. But I don't want to. *You're* my therapist now." Another twinge. "You know, I'm beginning to think things might work out."

"That's a good feeling."

Tears were in her eyes. Fell to the couch and cried for a while. When she was finished she sat up, blew her nose, and wiped her eyes with a tissue. "I feel very peaceful," she said. There was a rush of color in her face. Her eyelids drooped lazily and her half-pupils beamed with contentment. She sighed, "You know, I think I'm going to be okay. For the first time in my life I think I'm going to make it."

I guess I beamed back, hoping my anxiety wouldn't show.

That was an hour ago. Still have the anxiety tumbling inside me now. Wishing I'd had the chance to consult with her psychiatrist. Jennifer had asked me not to contact him, wanted to keep our therapy a secret. I had to respect her defenses, her privacy. At the end of today's session, she reiterated that she didn't want me to contact him. Afraid I'd be influenced by his negative attitude toward her and conspire with him.

Wondering where it's all going. Feels like I've gotten sucked into an emotional hurricane. Like I'm being pulled by Jennifer's longings, wrenched by the pain of her humiliations, tousled by her joy. She's a force field, the eye of the hurricane, soft blue knowing, watching, still-as-the-night eyes, following me everywhere. Making me think about her. Making me have fantasies about her. Fantasies of being so very nice to her, nice the way nobody ever was. Fantasies of giving her life a happy ending. Even fantasies of marrying her.

No, I tell myself. Don't think that way. I try to dismiss these thoughts from my jangling mind. They're the countertransference feelings and thoughts she's inducing in me. It's what she's wanted from all her past therapists, and why they came to feel overwhelmed by her, left her. It's her thoughts and feelings becoming my thoughts and feelings, her projective identification of me. Can feel her fear that I'll desert her if she trusts me too much, hear her saying, Don't let me down, don't let me down, don't let me down, do everything I ask or I'll feel let down! But it's my fault too. Shouldn't have taken her to Philadelphia. That encouraged the erotic transference, made her feel I was going to have an extratherapy relationship. Has the transference been irrevocably contaminated?

What makes it even more difficult is that in many ways she seems just the woman I've been looking for. Especially Mildred. She really wants me and thinks I'm great and good. We have much in common. Like her family, my family also scapegoated me, gave me the message I was no good, a clown, not very bright. If I'm her knight, she's also what I've always wanted in a woman. Sees me as good, bright, strong. So I ask myself, if I can get her integrated, wouldn't she make a good wife for me? With our like temperaments, backgrounds, talents, couldn't we be soulmates? Or is this a rationalization based on countertransference feelings? Don't know. Don't know.

S INCE SHE went off Thorazine she's been crying every session. Comes in three times a week now. (I offered to let her owe me for the third session.) Lies down on the couch without a word. Stamps her feet. Cries, "No! No! No!" and off she goes, while I sit on the chair watching over her.

"I can't stop crying," she says.

"That's good," I say.

"I don't understand," she says.

"Go with it," I say.

She trembles and gasps and cries some more, turning this way and that, flopping around on her belly, burying her face in the cushion, stopping to blow her nose, crying angrily, sadly, loudly, softly. The more she cries, the more memories rise to the surface, long entombed in clots of repressed emotion.

Today she got to the source of her habit of sitting on the floor. She had been crying for a while when she suddenly sat up. Winced, shook her head and looked at me.

"I just realized why I'm afraid of depending on you."

"Why?"

"I'm afraid of losing you." Her eyes focused inward for a moment. She hugged herself and looked lost and forlorn. Then she glanced up. "You know, a memory just flashed through my head. I remembered when I was very little, about three or four or five, and I used to sit in the closet. I used to sit there for hours, in the back of the hallway closet, just the way I'm sitting here now, with my legs folded. Maybe that's why I feel safer sitting on the floor in the corner. I used to hide there in the dark of the closet praying my mother wouldn't find me."

"Do you remember the first time you hid there?"

"No . . . yes . . . that's strange, it just came to me. The first time I hid there was after Mrs. Perkins died. She was a nice old lady who used to let me play with her cat and feed me cookies and milk. I used to stay up in her apartment all day—or as long as I could before my mother made me come home. She didn't like Mrs. Perkins. She didn't like anybody who liked me. My mother never told me when Mrs. Perkins died. I found out later. She told me she moved away. But I knew she wouldn't move away without saying goodbye to me. She wouldn't have done that. That was when I first sat in the closet—the day after my mother told me Mrs. Perkins moved away. I went up the stairs to her apartment and rang her bell but she didn't answer. I kept ringing her bell over and over. Then I went and sat in the closet. I never really got to say goodbye to her."

"You're saying it now," I said.

She fell in a heap and began sobbing loudly.

Mrs. Perkins is an important piece of the puzzle. Her presence explains how Jennifer managed to survive as well as she did in an insane environment. Mrs. Perkins was a ray of sun in the dungeon of terror that was her childhood. She was that essential witness to the abuse that was being done to her, a haven of reality on which her ego could find support and model itself and with whom she could identify. Her first dissociation into Jenny might well have been based on an identification with Mrs. Perkins. At least one ray of health and reality is an absolute minimum requirement for sanity. Without it Jennifer would probably have descended into schizophrenia.

Jennifer's depression over the impending loss of Henrietta, as well as over all the other losses in her life, can likewise be traced back to the loss of Mrs. Perkins. When Mrs. Perkins died, Jennifer felt unprotected. Moreover, her mother deprived her of the opportunity to mourn this loss. Bowlby, in his work with hospitalized children in England, has shown how such early losses can lead to life-long depression. Because Jennifer never had the chance to react to or mourn the loss of Mrs. Perkins, her ego didn't build up the kind of strength it needed to cope with future losses. This put her into a dilemma: she craved someone on whom she could depend, but dreaded the possible loss of that person, which she perceived would again leave her isolated and unprotected.

"That's a very important memory," I told her, and presented her with my interpretation of how the loss of Mrs. Perkins was related to her depression about, and fear of, losses.

"That sounds right," she said, nodding thoughtfully.

"And now you're experiencing that same fear of dependency and fear of loss in your relationship with me."

"Yes. . . ."

She broke into another round of sobs. Must have done about twenty hours of crying by now. Seems to be getting a little less depressed, a little more optimistic each day. Gait also a bit lighter, posture a bit less rigid. Satisfying for me to take part in the process, to see it happening, to help her attain, at long last, a little peace.

MARATHON SESSION

S O MUCH has happened this weekend it'll probably take a few minutes to have a marathon session. Jennifer had been crying nearly every day for three weeks and had been heading toward what I thought was some kind of major catharsis ever since she began therapy three months ago. Often she'd still be crying deeply at the end of her sessions, and I'd regretfully have to stop her. This happened again on Friday, so I asked if she'd like to come in on Saturday and have an all-day session. She did. The session ended up going into Saturday night. It wasn't that cathartic, but it allowed me to meet two more personalities, Tom and Jess.

It started Saturday at about noon while I was moving furniture around. I'd decided to change things and was in the midst of pushing my desk across the room when Jennifer arrived.

"Need some help?" she asked.

"Sure."

I began to notice something different as we teamed up to push the desk, then move two bookshelves to another wall. She (he?) was walking more rigidly, and his gait as he slid the bookshelves around, carried the books, and lifted a chair was decidedly masculine. Also observed that he seemed competitive toward me. Wanted to prove he could do this heavy work as well or better than I could. The expression on his face bore the inscrutability and sulkiness of a preadolescent boy. During the course of the work he knotted his hair in a bun, accenting his boyish appearance.

"Are you Tom?" I asked now and again.

He didn't answer. He worked silently, sulkily. Never

slowing his pace. Never making eye contact with me. If I said "Wait" he would wait; if I said "Let's move this," he'd immediately start to move it, whether I was ready or not.

"You're Tom, aren't you?"

"Does it matter?"

"Yes."

"Why?"

"Because if you're Tom there are some things I'd like to ask you." He busied himself putting books in the shelves. "I was wondering how old you are." No answer. "Margaret says you're nine years old. Is that right?"

"Maybe."

We finished moving things around in silence. Asked him if he wanted some coffee. Didn't answer. Made myself some and sat down in my chair. He was sitting in the other chair, hands in his pockets, staring sullenly at the floor.

"I think you're Tom," I said again.

"What if I am?" he finally answered.

"May I ask you some questions?"

"Do what you want."

"Can you remember the first moment you came into existence?"

"What of it?"

"Was it when your aunt from Ireland sent Jenny a doll, and her mother wouldn't let her play with it?" My hunch was that Jennifer developed a masculine personality in response to the trauma of not being able to play with the doll. "Is that when you first came out?"

"Could be."

"You came out right after her mother took away the doll?"

"What if I did?"

"Did you hate the doll?"

"It was a stupid doll."

"So you came out when Jennifer and Jenny were feeling sad about the doll."

"Stupid girls."

"You don't like talking very much, do you, Tom?"

"What's the point?"

He looked down at the floor in silence. Was moving his foot around on the rug, making an invisible drawing. I decided to let the silence go on until he spoke of his own accord. If I wanted him to open up, I'd have to wait for him to take the initiative. Several minutes passed. Observed him out the corner of my eyes. Could see him getting uncomfortable, switching his position in the chair, tensing his jaw as though he were chewing on something hard. He wanted to talk but he didn't want me to know he wanted to talk.

"Do you box?" he asked after a while without looking at me.

"I did when I was a kid. Just for fun."

"My father taught me how to box." Spoke in an angry, sulky voice, his words clipped, his lips pursed. Glared down at rug. Had a vengeful expression in his eyes, the vengefulness of deep frustrations, disappointments, betrayals. "We used to go out behind the house and box. He'd always beat me. He taught me how to play soccer too. Did you ever play soccer?"

"No, I never did."

"I was the goalie on my father's soccer team. He coached a peewee team. He told me, 'You're the son I always wanted.' Sure. Only nothing I ever did was good enough for him. If I let a ball go into the net he'd yell at me in front of everybody. Call me names. He was great to the other kids on the team. They loved him." He smiled bitterly. "They thought I was lucky to have him as a father. My dad doesn't know it but someday I'm going to beat him up."

"Did he actually box with you?"

"Oh, yeah. He didn't let up either. A couple of times I ended up with a bloody nose."

"No wonder you want to beat him up." I smiled but

he kept his gaze downward. Made me sad to visualize Jennifer as a little girl, trying so desperately to get some approval that she even put on boxing gloves with her father and let him beat her. Toughing it out with him until her nose was bloody. Made me disgusted to visualize a father so insecure that he had to beat up his own daughter to prove his manhood. Couldn't even let her win a match or two. More than disgusting. Tragic. "No wonder you're angry," I said, trying to strike an empathetic chord. "I'd like to beat him up too."

He didn't answer. Didn't want any pity from me. Sat sulking for a while. It was clear he hated his father, but it was also likely he identified with him. Imagined the father must have been like Tom, a bitter man. If Tom (and Jennifer) had not had the benefit of therapy, he might have grown up to abuse his (her) own son in a similar fashion.

"How do you like the work Jennifer's been doing?" I asked. Thought maybe a change of subject would bring new life to the conversation.

"What do you mean?"

"The therapy work."

"I don't care."

"Don't you think all the crying she's been doing is good for her?"

"That's sissy stuff."

"How does it feel to be the only male personality?"

"I don't like it. They give me a lot of flak."

"Who? Margaret? Mildred? Jennifer?"

"All of them. I had my hair cut a few years ago, in a crew cut. They all gave me flak about it. I can't do anything without being nagged."

Had to suppress a laugh at the thought of Jennifer, as Tom, being nagged by herself as Mildred, Margaret, Jess, Jenny, et al. "When did you get the crew cut?"

"After Jennifer got out of the hospital."

"Was that when she had the therapist who dropped her?"

"Yeah. She was in love with him. I thought he was dumb."

"What do you think of me?"

"I don't."

"You don't ever think of me?"

"Nope. Why should I?"

"You don't go in much for therapy either, I take it."

"What's the point?"

"To feel better."

"I'll feel fine after I beat up my dad."

"You'll feel even better when you become integrated with Jennifer and the others."

"I've got to take a crap."

Tom disappeared into the rest room and in a few minutes returned as Mildred. "Tom was upset by your questions," she said. Her hair was in a ponytail and there was a calm smile on her face.

"How've you been, Mildred?" I said. "I haven't seen you for a long while."

"I'm good." She went to the window and gazed at the sky. Stood with her hands clasped behind her back. Sticking out her behind. Reminded me of the session when she'd presented me with a mum. Must have been Mildred. Gazed at the hazy blue day, standing still and calm. I looked at her back and at the sky beyond her.

Early August. No cloud anywhere to filter the sun. No breeze to move the air. Children's voices coming from the park across the street. A siren in the distance. A happy day. A sad day. Another summer passing by. Another year out of my life and hers.

"And how are *you*?" she asked, turning around.

"Quite fine," I said.

"I guess we're both fine then." She ensconced herself on the couch.

"Looks that way."

"Yes, it does, doesn't it?"

Gave me one of her patented sidelong glances. Big

blue eyes. Eyes that seemed to know many secrets. Eyes that calmly waited for me to catch up to her.

"You're too much, Mildred," I said.

"I've always thought so. But it's always nice to hear somebody else confirm it."

I laughed. She really meant it.

"So, are you still working on Henrietta's biography?"

"Oh, yes."

"How's it going?"

"Slowly. I'm still editing the tapes, actually."

"Is it hard work?"

"Yes. But it's also quite exhilarating."

As I looked at her I thought, as I'd thought many times before, how extraordinary it was that Jennifer could have such a confident personality. When I was with her, I sometimes felt as though I should be the patient and she the therapist. She was so wise, endearing, engaging. Made me forget about doing therapy. "So you're enjoying it?"

"I find Henrietta's life fascinating. I find *her* fascinating. She had to escape from Germany when the Nazis took over and start her life all over again. Within a few years she rose to the top of her field. She had such courage."

"She does sound fascinating."

"And she was a marvelous role model. She set such a wonderful example for young women to follow."

"What made her a good role model?"

"In her quiet way she was a revolutionary. She went against the established tradition, but she did it in such a subtle way people didn't notice."

"You think she was a good role model because she went against the establishment?"

"Yes."

"Why is that so important?"

"Because the establishment is usually passé."

"I see." Something not right about her thinking. Decide to play the devil's advocate. "Then anybody who goes against the establishment is a good role model?"

"In a way, yes."

"How about Hitler? Was he a good role model?"

"Hitler?" She seemed surprised.

"Yes, Hitler," I said, smiling. "He went against the establishment in Germany. He and his Nazi party revolutionized Germany. Did that make Hitler a good role model? Was he a good role model for German youths?"

Didn't pause for a second. "Actually, sick as he was, Hitler was a role model."

"Would you care to explain?"

"At the time he came to power Germany was in a shambles. They'd lost World War I. There was widespread depression, crime, perversion. The young people of Germany had nobody to look up to, nobody to tell them how to get moving again."

"He sure showed them how to get moving."

"Yes, he did. He caused awful misery and destruction, he was certainly a sick man. But he also had a genius for motivating people. He revived the spirit of Germany, at least at first. He was a sick man, but as Voltaire said, 'Man is not born wicked; he becomes so as he becomes sick.'"

"You have an interesting way of arguing, Mildred."

"Thanks."

"I have a feeling you seldom lose arguments."

"Very seldom."

Had to admire her spunk. She spoke with such authority that her argument almost sounded logical. But of course it was absurd for me even to be having a debate about whether Hitler was a good role model. Such was her engaging personality that I'd been lured into it. Having caught myself, I looked into her earnest doelike eyes and had the thought that she was not real. I was having an illogical debate with an unreal person. "This is strange," I said, sharing my analysis of the situation. "I'm sitting here thinking to myself you're a figment of Jennifer's imagination. You're not real, Mildred. You're not listed in the telephone book, you're not counted in the census, you don't exist. You're Jennifer's unconscious. I'm talking about Hitler with Jennifer's unconscious."

She took it the way I thought she would. "I've got to admit that's funny," she said, laughing quietly.

"Speaking of Jennifer, is she around?"

"I'm trying to include her, but I'm not sure she wants to be."

"Who else is here? Is Jess here?" I was curious about this elusive, coquettish personality.

"She's here. But she doesn't want to come out."

"Why not?"

"Jess is very elusive. She only comes out when she wants to."

"Margaret said she was a tease."

"She's laughing at that."

"Jess? I want to talk to you."

"She's still laughing."

"I'm serious. Jess?"

Jess wouldn't come out. Too independent-minded. By then it was midafternoon, and Mildred and I went out to eat hamburgers at the corner coffee shop. Mildred ordered hers rare. Mine was well done. Sat by the window, watching people walk by. Made up stories about them. Mildred said of one man who had a goatee that he was probably a refrigerator repairman from Nutley, New Jersey, who secretly believed he was Freud. When we returned to the office I asked her if she could feel Jennifer inside her as she had during the drive to and from Philadelphia. She said she could. Then her face went from calm to confused.

"Jennifer?"

"Yes." She blinked and looked around.

"Have you been aware of what's been happening?"

"Sort of. I remember being Mildred. It was as if I were drugged. It reminded me of when I stopped seeing my psychiatrist, and Margaret was there . . . a curious feeling."

"It's really happening. You're becoming integrated."

I'd never witnessed anything like it before. You don't see such tangible and dramatic signs of change in an average patient. Nor such immediate ones. It was almost like watching an act of magic.

"Sometimes life feels so beautiful, so meaningful and rich with possibilities," she said, sitting back on the couch, her legs sprawled out in her faded jeans, her arms at her sides. Looking more relaxed than I'd ever seen her. Smiling with unobstructed joy. Letting her eyelids droop with exhaustion and relief. "I actually feel *lucky,* and that's strange, because I usually feel unlucky. I feel lucky to be here today. Lucky to know you." Smiled shyly.

"I feel lucky to know you, too."

"Do you really feel lucky?" she asked. "Why?"

"Why do you think?"

"Because I'm such a crazy patient?"

"You *are* challenging. But it's more than that." I'd gone this far. Might as well take a risk and stroke her a bit. She deserved it, after all the hard work she'd done. "You're an extremely interesting patient whose determination and courage I admire. I marvel at the pain you've faced and worked through in therapy, and at the way you've been able to throw yourself into the exercises with abandon. Frankly, I wasn't able to do that in my own therapy. Few people are."

And with that she began to cry. For the rest of the afternoon and into the early evening she alternately cried and talked, pouring forth new memories. Remembered how once her mother had forced her younger brother to have sex with her younger sister (this brother was now in prison). How her father had kicked down the bathroom door while she was taking a shower at the age of eleven and berated her. How her younger brothers and sisters turned on her and treated her just as her mother and father treated her. After a while she lay exhausted on the couch, her face in her arms, and I thought she was asleep. I went for a walk, my head spinning.

When I returned she was sitting in my easy chair, with its built-in footrest. Sat with her feet on the footrest, crossed at the ankles. Sneakers lying on the floor. Her hair hanging loosely around her shoulders, a few strands sensually covering her left eye. Had also put on dark red lipstick. Languishing in the chair, one arm curled around her head, the other holding one of my books, *Varieties of Sexuality*.

"Jess?" I asked, taking a seat on the couch.

"Who's Jess?" she replied with a straight face.

"You are."

"Am I?"

"Well, if you're not Jess, who are you?"

"I'm Jennifer."

"No, you're not."

"Okay, then I'm not Jennifer." She smiled coyly.

I shook my head. Watched her silently. She sat smiling like an imp, and there was an intensity about her that, as though fueled by some inner fire, gave her eyes a peculiar sheen. Could almost see flames in her pupils. Sat swaying to an imaginary tune, tapping her fingers to an imaginary rhythm, smiling about some secret joke as she thumbed through the book. If I'd diagnosed her, I would have put her down as a "manic."

"What're you reading?"

"Do you know anything about nymphomania?"

"A little. Why do you ask?"

"Just wondering." She tossed the book on the desk beside her. "Hey, would you like to play a fun game?"

"I must say, Jess, you're very different than the others."

"Of *course* I'm different. I'm me!" She smiled with her full intensity, cocking her head, glancing at me impishly from the corners of her eyes. "So. Do you want to play the game or not? It's a very easy game. We both make silly faces at the same time, and the first one who laughs loses."

"I used to play that when I was a kid."

"I'm still a kid. I hope I'll always be a kid."

"How old *are* you?"

"I thought you wanted to play?"

"Margaret said you were twenty-two. Is that right?"

"If she said so."

"Tell me."

"You're *sooooo* serious. Do you want to play or not?"

"All right. Let's play."

She moved the easy chair up close so her face was right near mine. Had absolutely no inhibition. Was sitting up on the chair hands-on-hips. Grinning at me. At first all I could do was fold my arms and stand my ground, awed that Jennifer could conjure up this kind of personality, so seemingly opposite to her own. This new personality crossed her eyes and puckered her lips like a fish. Opened and closed her nostrils. Smiled like an idiot, blinking her eyelids rapidly. Looked retarded, her eyes rolling back, her mouth falling open, her tongue to one side. Made a snoring noise. I kept stifling my impulse to laugh. Managed a few weak attempts at crossing my own eyes, wrinkling my face, raising my brows. Normally I'm no slouch in the clowning department, but when up against her mania I was intimidated into submission. I finally tossed up a laugh.

"I win! I win!" she squealed.

"You should be an actress."

"I know." She flickered her brows dramatically.

"Have you done any acting?"

"Have *I* done any acting? Have *I* done any acting? I'm acting all the time!"

"Seriously."

"You want *me* to be serious? I try never to be serious. It's bad for the health. Very, very bad. There are far too many serious people in the world. That's what's wrong with it, you know."

"Really, do you ever perform? Were you ever there, say, when Jennifer was dancing?" I was imagining what a combination they would be, with Jennifer's grace and vulnerability and Jess's comedic talents.

"Was I ever *there?*"

"Did you participate?"

"Yes, yes, yes! I participate *if* she's doing something I like. Something with personality, something with panache." She'd sat back in the chair again. Was swaying, tapping her fingers. "But most of the time Jennifer does these depressing, *depressing* pieces." Her voice dropped an octave on the word "depressing."

"Jess, may I ask you a question?"

"Oooooooh! You're going to be *serious* again. I can tell."

"Just one question."

"I know, I know. You want to ask me when I first appeared on this green earth, right?"

"Exactly."

"Aaaaaaah!" she moaned. Looked up at the sky, arms out. "Mommie, what is he *doing* to me? All right. If I answer your question will you stop being serious for the rest of the evening?"

"I promise."

"Cross your heart?"

"Cross my heart."

"I don't know *how* I get myself into these things." She sighed, sat back. "Okay. What is the question? Ask."

"The question was—"

"Oh, yes. WHEN DID JESS FIRST APPEAR?" She articulated each word as though narrating a documentary. "JESS FIRST APPEARED ON THIS GREEN, BUT DYING, EARTH IN THE SUMMER WHEN JENNIFER WAS TWELVE YEARS OLD."

"What happened then?"

"Oh, *no!* I already answered your question. You don't get to ask another one."

"This is the second part of my question. It's all one question."

"You lie like a dog!"

"Just this one question, then I won't be serious anymore."

"That's what you said before."

"What happened when Jennifer was twelve?"

"You're *sooooo* persistent! Okay, I'll tell you what happened." She spoke with mock-annoyance. "A coat-hanger abortion. That's what happened."

"Jennifer had a coat-hanger abortion?"

"No, silly. She witnessed one. It happened to a friend of hers."

"And that's when you first appeared?"

"I was there for the abortion. But I didn't really *come out*—if you know what I mean—until a few nights later."

"What happened a few nights later?"

"That's three questions. Remember that. You have to play three games afterwards. Promise?"

"I promise. What happened a few nights later?"

"I'm *going* to tell you. Relax. What happened a few nights later? That's when Jennifer's father caught her and a neighborhood boy in his basement. They weren't doing anything, really. Just a little fooling around, innocent kissing. But her father thought they had been HAVING SEX. So he went slightly crazy, took her home, threw her on the floor, beat her, kicked her, and called her some wonderful names like whore, slut, and tramp."

"Was it you who was in that basement?"

"You got it! You're very bright!"

"And it was you who came out at the wedding and flirted with Jennifer's sister's boyfriend."

"Right again! Okay, that's it. That's all the questions. My turn."

"Very interesting. So it would seem you represent Jennifer's repressed sexuality."

"Oooooooh! Must we analyze?"

"What's wrong with analyzing?"

"Analysis, schmalysis! Life is to be lived, not analyzed. Ready for another game?" She smiled, raising and lowering her brows.

I laughed. "All right. Let's play."

She moved closer. Began making faces.

"Is Jennifer here now?" I asked.

"I'm Jennifer."

"No, really. Are you aware of Jennifer inside of you? Is she aware of what's going on now?"

"Oooooooh! You're no fun."

"Weren't you the one who wrote in the letter to Jennifer that you wanted to have a miraculous cure so you could make love with me?"

She groaned. "You had to bring that up." Smiled coyly. "Yes, I believe I did write that. Why?"

"If you're really interested in a miraculous cure, then you should begin letting Jennifer be aware of you."

"Suppose I do? Then what?"

"Then you'll be on the way to a cure."

"And then?" She blinked, grinning.

"Then you'll find a nice man and live happily ever after."

"Boring. Let's play another game. I thought you said you wanted to play another game? Stop jabbering and play."

JESS AND I played another game. Afterward I wanted to ask her more questions, but she vanished as quickly as she had appeared. By this time it was around midnight.

Then Jennifer was there, claiming to have a faint recollection of being Jess. Talked for a while about her hopes of returning to the world of dance, then I looked at my watch and said, "I think we'd better call it a night."

"Thanks for this extended session," she said. "I really appreciate it, and please send me a bill. I will pay for it as soon as I can."

"Whenever."

Walked her home. Awkward moment standing in front of her building. Had an internal monologue: to make physical contact or not to make physical contact. Finally hugged her self-consciously. Her lips grazed my cheek. She blushed, ran into her building. I trudged home, wondering about transference and love.

If Jennifer thinks I'm kind, I thought, is that strictly transference? If Jess wants to make love "with that man," has she simply eroticized her adolescent longing for a Good Daddy? If Mildred appreciates my mind, is she idealizing me? If I feel deeply touched, attracted to, and interested in Jennifer, is that strictly countertransference, or is there some real affection for the truly fantastic human being Jennifer is?

It's now 3:00 A.M. Sunday. I've been writing since 1:00 A.M. Getting drowsy. Can't think any longer. Eyelids feel like sandpaper. Good night.

I'D EXPECTED that when Jennifer came in last Monday she'd have a lot of thoughts and feelings about the weekend. Instead, she was despondent again about Henrietta. Henrietta had passed away Sunday night. Took three sessions of crying to get things back to where they were during the marathon.

Today she seemed to reach bottom. Got in touch with her anger at Henrietta, then her anger at Mrs. Perkins, then her anger at her mother, all in quick succession. Went full cycle back to Henrietta, this time with sadness and nostalgia. Remembered traveling with her to Paris. Doing a dance duet. Taking dance classes taught by her. And the hours they spent together in her apartment on Riverside Drive, where Jennifer tape-recorded her memoirs. "We used to sit by her fireplace and drink tea. She had a huge antique fireplace with a mantelpiece of carved oak. We both loved antique furniture. She had such a soft, gracious manner. She could keep you spellbound for hours. But she could listen too. She was the first person I ever felt really *listened* to me."

By the end of today's session, she had begun to make her peace with Henrietta's death. "You know, I feel lucky because I'll always have the memories of loving her. They can never take *them* away." She gave me one of her droopy-lidded smiles of relief.

"That's right," I affirmed.

Glad Henrietta has finally passed away. Her lingering death had been hanging over us. Now we can move on.

BRUNCH WITH MARY

HAD BEEN trying to convince the last of Jennifer's six alter personalities to come out for some time, without success. Mary was the most reclusive one, and the most resistant to therapy. Absolutely refused to come to my office. Using Mildred as a go-between, I negotiated with Mary and finally got her to agree to meet me for brunch at her favorite restaurant, Jimmy's, on the Upper East Side. Mildred prompted me on what to talk with her about. "Remember, she likes the finer things, and she's very sensitive."

Jimmy's was a place with stained glass windows, white cotton tablecloths, and potted palms arching out from the corners. When I arrived she was already seated at "her table," in a corner next to one of the palms. Shook hands with me quite formally, rising from her chair. Sat down in a prim, ladylike manner and ordered her French omelette with savoir-faire. There was an uncomfortable silence.

"Mildred tells me you're interested in art and anthropology."

"Yes, that is correct."

Pause.

"And you like going to museums."

"Yes, I like going to museums very much."

Pause.

"And you like dining in fine restaurants, obviously."

"Yes."

Mary was, to say the least, not a conversationalist. As we ate, I took notice of her manner. Sat across from me stiffly, formally, apparently always concerned about her poise. Lifted a forkful of eggs daintily to her mouth, chewed it carefully and slowly. I counted exactly twenty chews per forkful. With the other hand she regularly brought her napkin to her lips and gave them a gentle dab. Glanced at me as she ate, furtively, then looked away. Didn't want to be so rude as to stare. Clothing just right: a dark blue spring suit, nylon stockings, white blouse. Eyeliner and lipstick of a conservative brown shade. White gloves, which she'd removed when we started to eat and placed neatly on the table beside her plate.

"Mary, may I ask you a question?"

She put down her fork and finished chewing before answering. "Certainly."

"When did you first come into existence? Mildred thought it was on the day after Jennifer was forced to sell her antique furniture and move into a roominghouse."

"That is not entirely correct," she said. "I did appear on that particular day. I sensed that Jennifer needed me to take charge of things. But I had, to be precise, appeared a few days earlier, briefly. It was then she first realized she would have to move out and sell her furniture."

"I see. Tell me, do you consider yourself Jennifer's sister?"

"No." A bemused smile flickered on her face. "I am a good friend."

"You seem to have an accent."

"Yes. How discerning of you to notice. I was born in England."

"And how did you come to meet Jennifer?"

"My family moved to New York a year before I met Jennifer."

"So you're Jennifer's rich friend?"

"You might put it that way."

Another pause.

"I understand you also know a lot about antiques."

"Yes, I very much enjoy shopping for antiques."

Another pause.

"And opera. I understand you like opera."

"Yes, that is so."

"Do you have any favorites?"

"I have a great many favorites."

Another pause.

"Do you like Puccini?"

"Yes, very much."

Another pause.

The conversation continued in this stilted manner. Found myself feeling restless, wanting to get away. Of all seven personalities, Mary seemed the most pathetic. All the other personalities possessed some kind of vitality that redeemed them. Mary lacked this. What came across was a powerful sadness and resignation masked only flimsily by a veneer of formality. The veneer wasn't convincing. She was the least believable of Jennifer's personalities. Had the appearance of a child playacting a princess and not quite being able to carry it off. The other personalities were "truly" other people. Distinct creatures with no trace of Jennifer in them. Not Mary.

She continued to avoid my eyes. Then it struck me that perhaps she was avoiding my eyes because she was aware of her own transparency. Was she the least perfectly formed personality, or had the process of integration already affected her too? Was that Jennifer's sadness and resignation in Mary's eyes? Was that Jennifer's despair in the back of her voice?

THE MEETING with Mary left me full of excitement. Thought about her and the other personalities all day Sunday. Did more theorizing about personality formation. Even made a chart delineating the character structures of each of the personalities. Mildred came in today, and the first thing I did was sit her down to show her the chart.

"What's this?" she asked.

"I've charted Jennifer's personalities." I sat down on the couch beside her. "What do you think?"

Her brows knitted. She squinted her eyes. Laid it aside. "It's nice."

"That's all, just nice?"

"I don't know if I understand it."

"I'll explain it to you." I was so intent on showing her the chart and giving her my interpretation of it that I failed to recognize the rather depressed mood she was in. She was not at all her usual calm, cheerful self, but I didn't notice until later. Took the chart in my hand and held it before us. Had drawn seven circles, a large one in the center and six smaller ones surrounding the large one. The central circle contained a description of Jennifer's character traits, while the others contained descriptions of her alter personalities. I'd also provided information on when each of the personalities first appeared. "What do you think?" I asked again.

"It's . . . interesting." Seemed disturbed by the chart. Eyes flitting here and there at the facts and figures as though she was afraid they might contaminate her.

JENNIFER
and her personalities

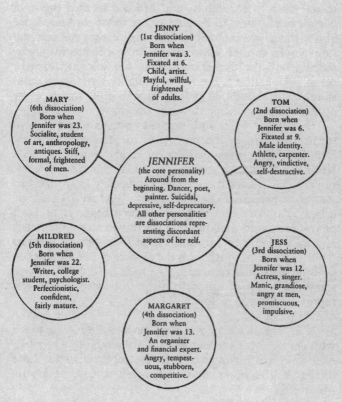

JENNY
(1st dissociation)
Born when
Jennifer was 3.
Fixated at 6.
Child, artist.
Playful, willful,
frightened
of adults.

MARY
(6th dissociation)
Born when
Jennifer was 23.
Socialite, student
of art, anthropology,
antiques. Stiff,
formal, frightened
of men.

TOM
(2nd dissociation)
Born when
Jennifer was 6.
Fixated at 9.
Male identity.
Athlete, carpenter.
Angry, vindictive,
self-destructive.

JENNIFER
(the core personality)
Around from the
beginning. Dancer, poet,
painter. Suicidal,
depressive, self-deprecatory.
All other personalities
are dissociations repre-
senting discordant
aspects of her self.

MILDRED
(5th dissociation)
Born when
Jennifer was 22.
Writer, college
student, psychologist.
Perfectionistic,
confident,
fairly mature.

JESS
(3rd dissociation)
Born when
Jennifer was 12.
Actress, singer.
Manic, grandiose,
angry at men,
promiscuous,
impulsive.

MARGARET
(4th dissociation)
Born when
Jennifer was 13.
An organizer
and financial expert.
Angry, tempest-
uous, stubborn,
competitive.

"As you can see, Mary was the sixth dissociation, just as we speculated. She confirmed on Saturday she was around when Jennifer was forced to move into the roominghouse. When Jennifer felt most impoverished she conjured up a rich and cultured alter ego."

"That doesn't really surprise me."

"Having met Mary, I feel I have a fairly complete

grasp of how all the personalities got formed." I launched into a summation of my findings. Had an inexorable need to tell them to somebody, and Mildred seemed the right person to tell them to because of her thirst for knowledge about things psychological. Also hoped that the summation would further advance the cause of integration by seeping into the farther reaches of her unconscious (the other personalities). She listened attentively enough, considering her mood. Sat prettily though a bit wanly, every now and then glancing down at the chart.

I outlined when and how each personality had been formed, as well as the process of identification of each. Explained how each personality compensated for what Jennifer lacked, and how the particular traumatic circumstances that triggered each alter personality led to the formation of particular character traits. "You see," I said resolutely, "all the pieces of the puzzle have begun to fit. Each of you represents qualities that are threatening to Jennifer, and each of you performs a certain function. And just as Jennifer is out of touch with the aspects of herself that her other personalities represent, so also each of the other personalities is out of touch with the qualities that the rest represent. Do you follow?"

"I think so."

"In fact, none of the alter personalities is in touch with her feelings of tenderness and vulnerability. Only Jennifer feels that. Not even you are in touch with those things. You've never allowed yourself to cry, have you, Mildred?"

"No, I haven't."

"I didn't think so."

"So? What does that mean?"

"It means that in a sense each of the alter personalities is a stereotype."

"I'm a stereotype? Thanks."

"I didn't mean it that way. I'm just trying to explain that all of the personalities are delimited because they're all parts of the whole but not the whole. Each personality is a manifestation of infantile derivatives from early childhood. Each became fixated at a certain stage of development. Each developed particular ways of defending herself, and in the case of Tom, himself. And because of all these factors, each is stereotypical. Most people are stereotypes. Most people are caught in one mode or another, and have typical ways of behaving and defending themselves. They're fixed at an early age and act innocently like Jenny. They're stuck in a bitter and revengeful mode like Tom or an obsessive-compulsive mode like Margaret or a manicky mode like Jess. They're like a record with a crack in it, which has to go round and round that groove with the crack in it forever."

"And how am I stereotypical?" Mildred asked. "What defense do I use?"

"You? You use an intellectual defense. You use your intellect to defend against and to deny Jennifer's depression, Tom's bitterness, and Margaret's rage. Actually, though, I happen to think you're the least stereotypical of all the personalities. You're much more than an intellectual. But there's still a stereotypical quality about you, insofar as you're not able to be really aggressive and, as I pointed out before, you're not in touch with your vulnerability and tenderness."

"You don't think I can be aggressive. I'll remember that."

"Oh, no. What have I gotten myself into now."

"What about men? Are *they* stereotypes too?"

"Of course men are stereotypes. I've been talking about women, except for Tom, because I'm talking about Jennifer's personalities. I'm stereotypical, although I hate to admit it. I've repressed many parts of myself. I'm out of touch with my tenderness and sadness too. Like Margaret, I often tend to defend against my fears by taking an angry and aggressive stance."

"I haven't seen that side of you."

"Be thankful! Anyway, the point isn't that women or men are stereotypical. *People* are stereotypical. In fact, I just had the thought the other day that the reason writers are able to capture the characters they portray is because of that very fact. Most people are stereotypical. Throughout the history of literature there are certain character types that appear again and again. The proud but vain beauty. The coquette. The shy, withdrawn maiden. The mad scientist. The ladies' man. The sensitive but moody artist. These are all stereotypes. Indeed, many of the great characters of literature are stereotypes. They're fixed in a particular mode of being."

"That sounds true."

"I also had another thought about character formation. This is a little off the track, Mildred, and doesn't directly pertain to Jennifer. But since you're interested in psychology, I thought you'd like to hear it. Are you familiar with the twin studies they've done with schizophrenics?"

"Yes, I've read about them."

"What these researchers are saying, basically, is that if both identical twins raised from birth in differing family systems become schizophrenic, this proves that schizophrenia is inherited. It proves, they contend, that at least this form of personality formation is in the genes. Some researchers also contend psychotic depression is also inherited. But when we look at multiple personalities, what do we see? Several different personalities all developing in the same person, each personality resulting from a different traumatic circumstance. And one or two of the personalities might be diagnosed as depressive or schizophrenic. Jennifer, for example, would be diagnosed as suffering from depression, Margaret from obsessive-compulsion, Tom from borderline personality disorder, Jess from mania. Mary might be seen as a schizoid personality. Jenny possibly as an agoraphobic, someone who's afraid of open spaces."

"And what am I?"

"A mild hysteric."

"I'm glad you said mild."

"The point is that the personalities of a multiple personality are all quite separate character formations, each with its own IQ, talents, blood pressure, mannerisms, and the like, and each with its own psychopathology. Yet each has developed in the same person. Clearly nurture, not nature, caused them. In reading the literature on multiples I've found that it's quite common for them to be misdiagnosed as schizophrenic, manic-depressive, and the like. Research has shown that ninety-seven percent of multiples have been abused, sexually or in some way physically, before the age of three. There have always been those people throughout our history who have wanted to believe all so-called mental illnesses is inherited, even multiple personality. Indeed, in olden days, multiples were seen as possessed by the devil and burned at the stake as witches. We don't want to take responsibility for the dark side of our nature. We don't want to take responsibility for parental cruelty and societal psychopathology. If there's evil or mental sickness in the world, maybe God or the devil put it there. We had nothing to do with it."

"That's a good point."

"Another thing about those twin studies is they don't prove conclusively that schizophrenia is inherited. All they prove is that twins raised in separate environments often become schizophrenic. What is not adequately accounted for in these studies is the effect of the mother's body chemistry on the fetus during pregnancy. Some psychoanalysts believe—and I subscribe to this theory—that the degree of psychopathology in an individual corresponds to the degree of repressed rage inside them. Therefore, a schizophrenic would have the greatest amount of repressed rage. Do you understand what the implications of this are? Imagine what it would do to one's body chemistry if one were chronically in a severe rage throughout one's lifetime? And imagine what would happen if a mother was full of repressed rage during pregnancy? This rage would be transmitted to the child, who would be born with an equal amount of repressed rage. This may account for the so-called predisposition to schizophrenia which psychiatrists often mention in these twin studies. If this theory is correct, schizophrenia is not inherited through the genes, but biologically and environmentally transmitted *in utero*.

"Freud once made an interesting comment about this nature-nurture debate in a letter he wrote to somebody. Wait a minute, I think I have it in my library." I pulled the book out of my shelf and found the quote. "Yes, here it is. He says, 'The question as to which is of greater significance, constitution or experience . . . can in my opinion only be answered by saying that fate and chance are not one or the other decisive. Why should there be an antithesis, since constitution after all is nothing but the sediment of experiences from a long line of ancestors.' You see, in a way Freud's word 'sediment' might also be seen as suggestive of this biological transmission I'm talking about. It might be a case of generations of mothers, each bearing a quantity of repressed rage that becomes transformed into schizophrenic body chemistry, which may in turn be transmitted to the growing fetus and even progressively influence the makeup of the genes themselves."

"That's an interesting idea."

I hurried on. "Anyway," I said, tossing the book aside, "in Jennifer's case it's pretty clear that all of her personalities were environmentally produced. And in a way, I think she's lucky."

"Lucky?"

"Yes, lucky to have managed to keep alive and intact all the various aspects of herself. She didn't repress them the way most people do. Instead she dissociated herself from them. Instead of repressing her rage, her sexuality and her various other qualities, she kept them alive in her dissociated personalities. So we don't have to dig up her unconscious, we just have to introduce her to her other personalities and integrate them with her. A process that's already begun."

I had run out of energy. Perhaps I'd said everything I wanted to say. Also I had taken a good look at her face, and all at once saw the sadness I'd avoided seeing up until then. "How does all this grab you?" I asked.

"It's fascinating," she said wistfully. "I can't refute anything you've said."

"You can't?"

"No."

"Then you agree about the necessity of integration?"

"Yes, I'm beginning to agree with that too—unfortunately."

"Unfortunately?"

"Yes. . . ."

She gazed off and it hit me how much like Jennifer she looked. Had Jennifer's sad, distracted, agitated appearance. Was much more vulnerable. A shadow in her eyes. A wrinkle in her brow. An arch in her back. Had even begun to rub her palms against her thighs a bit as Jennifer had done.

"What's the matter?" I asked.

She sighed. A Jennifer-like sigh. "Oh . . . just . . . you know . . . integration."

"What about it?"

"Just that . . . I'm worried about it."

"What worries you?"

"As I said, I'm beginning to agree with you that it's necessary. But I'm also afraid of it." Looked at me apologetically. "I've been feeling Jennifer inside me stronger and stronger. I can feel her trembling inside me now. It's not a good feeling. I feel very sad. Afraid . . . and sad."

"What do you feel afraid and sad about?"

"I'm afraid . . . I'm going to die. I know you've said that integration is some kind of combining of Jennifer and me, but I'm really feeling as though I'm dying. I'm afraid if integration *does* happen and we all become parts of Jennifer, then we'll all have to die. We won't be, you know, our own personalities anymore. That's why I'm sad. I really don't want to die. I like myself and I don't want to die."

I slid away from Mildred, sitting back on the couch in shock. Had not thought of it that way before. It was not just the fact of her possible death that touched me, but the matter-of-fact way in which she spoke of it.

"You look so very sad," she said, leaning close to me.

I looked into her intelligent, unassuming eyes and became aware of how deep my feelings were about her. Had never thought about her not being around anymore. Integration had been mainly an abstract concept. "I guess I never realized how much I care about you, Mildred," I said, looking at her, trying to fix her in time. Maybe integration wasn't the only way, I thought. She gave me one of her knowing smiles, as though sharing my thoughts. I felt a tear slide down my cheek. "I'm going to miss you, Mildred," I said. "I'm really going to miss you."

HAD INSOMNIA last night. Still trying to think of a way to avoid losing Mildred. Started thinking that perhaps Jennifer was better off as a multiple personality. Who was I to tamper with her character structure? Was I playing God?

When Mildred came again today I told her what I'd been thinking. "I've had some thoughts about integration. Actually, I've been obsessing about it since Monday. I'm not so sure integration is best."

"You're sweet," she said, tears coming into her eyes. "You're the sweetest man I've ever met."

"No, just selfish. I don't want to lose you."

With that she sank into herself and rolled into a ball on the couch. Began to tremble and cry as Jennifer had once trembled and cried. Sobbing with her entire body. Shaking her head. Wincing. Then she lay on her belly and cried with her face in the cushion, as Jennifer had often done. Lifted her head every now and then to gasp for air. Sobbing violently. When she had drained herself, she sat up again, and there was Jennifer's dazed expression and rueful blue eyes.

"What . . . day is it?"

"Wednesday. Hello, Jennifer."

"Wednesday . . . ?" She looked around at the objects of my office. "Oh, my . . . this is strange. . . ." She kept looking around. Finally stopped and focused on me, pointedly. "This is really strange. . . ."

"What's strange?"

"I hear . . . a voice inside me. It's telling me to say I'm Mildred."

"Really?" I'd been trying to get Jennifer to say she was Mildred and Mildred to say she was Jennifer for a few weeks. It was a Gestalt therapy technique. Hadn't worked previously. Now I knew it would. "Then say it."

She gaped at me. "Should I?" She had an odd smile— a smile mixed with joy, sadness, and incredulity.

"Say it!"

"I'm . . . Mildred. . . ."

"Well? How does it feel?"

"Strange. . . ." A smile of puzzlement.

"Now say 'I'm Jennifer.' "

"I'm Jennifer."

When she'd said "I'm Mildred," she looked like Jennifer. When she said "I'm Jennifer," she looked like Mildred. Then she began to alternate from one to another.

"It feels . . . really strange. . . ." she said, looking like Jennifer.

"I'll second that," Jennifer said, looking like Mildred.

She had become a creature with two faces. "This is incredible," I said. "I wish you could see yourself now. I wish I had a video camera so I could capture this. How does it feel? Do you feel integrated? Together?"

"I'm not sure. . . ." Jennifer said.

"I think so," Mildred said.

"But you *are* aware of each other? You're both aware of each other's feelings and so forth, right?"

"Yes, I think so. . . . Yes, definitely!"

INITIALLY IT seemed odd to me that the moment I stopped pushing for integration, that was when Mildred and Jennifer became integrated. But on second thought it seemed quite understandable. The most therapeutic thing a therapist can do is accept a patient as is. By accepting a patient as is, you help her to accept herself. Only when a person accepts herself as is can she change. In order to stop being sad, one must accept one's sadness. In order to stop being a multiple personality, one must accept one's multiple personalities. If I hadn't accepted her personalities, they would have gone back into hiding, grown more entrenched. What one resists grows larger. What one accepts goes away. So it had been with Mildred and Jennifer.

My pen feels as if it's vibrating as I write this. Feel excited, joyful, sad, drained, and relieved, all at the same time. Excited and joyful to have witnessed this process of change. Sad not knowing what will happen to Mildred. Drained by my overinvolvement in this case. Relieved that it's coming to some kind of culmination. For a while now I've been feeling impatient about achieving integration. As involved as I am, there have also been thoughts about wanting to get away from her. At least for a while.

Still trying to sort things out. Has occurred to me that integration may be happening so quickly because of her expectations. As Jess wrote, "We have to have a miraculous cure because I want to make love with this man." What does Mildred expect? Jennifer? Jenny? The others? Now that I've regressed Jennifer and brought out her infantile thoughts and impulses, will I be able to successfully interpret them? Seems like she keeps wanting more and more.

PART

III

~⁓~

JENNIFER'S DIARY

JENNIFER, AUGUST 13

I DON'T want to write this. i don't know what to say.
Gerry says i should keep a diary—he showed me the
one he's keeping. He says it will help me understand
myself. i don't know if i want to.

i miss Henrietta. Miss her terribly. She was such a big
part of who i am today. i don't know what i would have
done had i not met her. Can't walk down a street without
having a memory of her. i'm trying to store all the good
memories inside me, for comfort and strength.

i don't know what to say. i'm not much of a writer—
more of a visual person. i prefer to dance or paint, tho
sometimes i write poetry, but that doesn't feel like writing,
more like word painting. When i'm dancing or painting i
feel good about myself. When i'm not i feel inadequate.

i'm not sure what Gerry wants me to write. i think he
wants me to write about integration, about Mildred and i
becoming integrated, and how i feel about it. i don't know
why i'm avoiding that—i guess i still feel resistant to integration—feel frightened of i don't know what. Gerry says
whenever i want to say "i don't know" i should say "i
don't want to know," so i take responsibility for my feelings. All right, i don't want to know what i'm afraid of.

i hear Mildred's voice inside my head now, telling me
"You're afraid of your sexual feelings," and i guess that's
true. It's been terribly difficult being aware of Mildred's
(my?) sexual feelings. It's frightening and confusing—both
my parents made me feel it was wrong to have sexual
feelings and now Mildred's telling me it's okay. And she's
telling me i'm afraid of integration because i'm afraid to be
all the things my parents told me not to be. i'm not sup-

posed to be educated, either. Mildred is educated. My father hated anybody with a college diploma—never finished high school—had to work from the age of eleven.

i remember my father constantly putting down my grandmother because she had graduated from college. She came from a long line of intellectuals, doctors, lawyers, and architects. He thought intellectuals were jerks—if he was watching TV and saw anybody who looked as if they were too intellectual, he'd carry on in such a way that nobody else could enjoy the program.

Mildred has a college education, although she hasn't actually received her degree yet. Now that i've gotten in touch with her, i'm receiving all sorts of new information in my head about her. It's terribly strange to feel her feelings and think her thoughts—even more strange to accept that those feelings and thoughts are mine. i still can't believe she and i are one—i know Gerry won't want to read this, but it's true. i still feel we're separate people, although i hear her thoughts and feel her feelings. It's hard to believe she is really a part of me. If my father ever found out what Mildred was thinking or feeling, he'd have a fit.

i feel terribly confused. Are Mildred's sexual feelings about Gerry really my own? i don't want to take responsibility for them. i shouldn't have those kinds of feelings about my therapist. i don't feel comfortable having sexual feelings about anybody, for that matter. i feel terribly vulnerable when i feel sexual toward a man. i'm afraid of becoming dependent on a man and then losing him. Sooner or later he'll find out i'm no good.

Gerry thinks that Mildred and i are integrated, because yesterday i heard Mildred's voice telling me to say she and i were one. i said it and she said it, but i don't feel integrated—whatever that is. When Mildred is talking i feel as if i'm conscious of her talking—as if i'm listening from somewhere inside of her. But i don't feel i'm her.

i guess i feel Mildred still doesn't accept parts of me, and i can't accept parts of her. She can't accept my depression, my feelings of inadequacy. She likes to think of herself as an up person. Neither of us is ready to totally integrate. (Is that all right, Gerry?)

It feels as though everything is happening terribly fast. Before i met Gerry i hardly ever cried—now i've been crying all the time. i can't stop now if i want to. i feel and recall so many things. i'm starting to feel better now, and it's scary to feel better. Why?

It's difficult to accept Gerry's positive feelings toward me—deep down i feel as if i'm no good. i have terrible thoughts and i hear voices and i sometimes i think i'm crazy. i don't know if Gerry really knows me. (i don't want to know if Gerry really knows me.) i wrote a poem about it.

> You say i'm cute and you say i'm nice
> i must really have you fooled
> running brick walls only work in China
> if anyone knew what was going on here
> they would have me locked away
>
> the war is on and the bombs are falling
> fragmenting time and space
> i am responsible for repairing the gaps
> i am trying to believe the talk that's going
>   around—but—
> i am still dreading tomorrow.

MILDRED, AUGUST 14

GERRY REALLY helped me to experience my/Jennifer's sadness, and the surprising thing about it is it's not so terrible as I imagined it would be. When I saw his tears on Wednesday, and he didn't seem embarrassed by it, it somehow made it all right for me to feel sad too. Gerry's so genuine. I am very much in love with him. I have never met such a loving, caring man. No matter what happens between us in the future, I'll always be grateful for what he's done for all of us.

I'm in agreement with Jennifer about our not being able to completely accept each other yet. It's true. I still have problems with accepting her depression. It is so overwhelming. I can accept feelings of sadness, but not of depression. I'm afraid that in accepting her depression as my own, I'll lose my good, fun qualities. I've always prided myself on my optimism, peace of mind, and sense of humor, as well as on my ability to flourish even under the most debilitating circumstances. I've learned to be philosophical about life, to make the best of it. To paraphrase the famous saying, I've learned to change that which can be changed, accept that which cannot be changed, and to tell the difference between the two. I'm dreading the thought of losing this quality when/if I merge with Jennifer completely.

However, it does seem that integration is inevitable. I'm not quite sure why—I suppose it must have a lot to do with our work with Gerry—but I find myself feeling more and thinking more of what Jennifer feels and thinks. Additionally, I have become less aware of what the others are thinking and feeling. Since Monday I've almost lost touch with them, whereas I used to be able to tune in whenever I liked.

It's unusual for me to be afraid of anything. As I said, I'm pretty much of an optimist. But I find I'm having recurring fears of death. I suppose I'm still resisting, as Gerry would put it. I'd like to cooperate with Gerry, but I'm afraid of losing myself, who *I* am. It really seems as if I were slowly dying, slowly being devoured by Jennifer's depression.

When I/we saw Gerry today I asked him about these concerns.

"Guess what?" I said. "I think we're still not completely integrated."

"Oh? How do you know?" he asked. He seemed disappointed.

"It feels as if we still haven't accepted each other's feelings."

"Is Jennifer there?" he asked.

"Yes, I'm here," I heard myself say, as Jennifer, and at the same time my entire body, from limb to limb, began trembling. "And I feel scared."

"What are you scared of?" Gerry asked.

"I don't know," Jennifer said. "I'm scared of integration. Scared of Mildred's feelings."

"Of her sexual feelings?"

"Maybe. I don't know."

I told Jennifer I wanted to ask Gerry something and she went away and allowed me to return. "I'd like to ask you something," I said. "Actually, I'd like to ask you three questions."

"Mildred?"

"Yes. It's me again. The first question—will I become Jennifer? Do you know what I mean?"

"You mean, will you, Mildred, disappear altogether?"

"Yes."

"I don't think so. I'm a novice at this myself, you know. But I don't think so." Gerry's honesty is one of his endearing qualities. "My understanding of it is that the first step of integration is a kind of co-consciousness, where you remain separate personalities but are aware of each other. Eventually you become completely integrated, like two colors merging, like red and blue forming purple. Think of it this way—you're not losing a Mildred, you're gaining a Jennifer."

"That's a good way to think about it." I laughed. "Next question. How come I've lost the capacity to tune in on the other personalities?"

"Have you? That's interesting. I suppose it's because you're no longer part of Jennifer's unconscious. You're now part of her conscious mind."

That made me feel much calmer. He was able to put things in perspective for me.

"The third question isn't really a question," I said. "I just want to say thanks for crying on Monday. That's what finally put me in touch with my own sadness."

"I'm glad."

Gerry is such a sensitive man. I've never met anybody like him. His understanding, acceptance and emotional support have been so important to all of us. He's the first man—the first person—who has ever known me. The irony of it is that he'll apparently also be the last. I love his facial expressions, too. Sometimes he can have such a stern, forbidding look that you can feel his eyes penetrating you and you want to run and hide. At other times he has such a look of innocence, you wonder how he could be a therapist at all. He's sort of like Charlie Chaplin trying to be a therapist.

I do have problems with his anger. He has his own blocks which, he says, he will have to work through in his own therapy, and—in terms of my/our relationship with him—I feel leery of that. He has a lot of anger, superficially, about women, but actually about his mother. He's pretty aware of it, though—how else would I know about it?—and I'm sure he'll "work it through." Anyway, that's only one part of him, and I try not to focus on the negative in people. The angry part of him is like Jennifer's Tom personality or Margaret.

Speaking of which, I've recently had this recurring fantasy of how Margaret and Tom could work off some of their anger and resentment at the parents. (Actually, I'm beginning to think of them more as my parents now.) The idea is to take the picture off of the piano, the one of Mum and Dad kissing, and paste it on the dart board in the kitchen. Tom and Margaret—and the rest of us too!— could throw darts at it. I can feel the Jennifer part of me trembling over this. She's afraid Dad will find out somehow and take revenge on her/us. I don't know why, but I've never been afraid of him.

All in all, I still feel optimistic, in spite of my fears of integration and death. I still have a feeling everything's going to be fine.

ALL DAY long I've been having two separate feelings about everything. At one moment I have the old feeling of doom, and at the next moment I feel optimistic. For example, I was walking through Central Park this morning after leaving Gerry and saw a woman walking her dog, and the Mildred part of me thought it was such a sweet, warm, frisky puppy and wanted to pet it, while the Jennifer part of me thought it was an evil dog and was scared of it. It's been that way about everything. I can't so much as buy an ice cream cone without getting into an internal debate about the harmfulness of sugar. It's really strange—I never knew I had so many feelings, opinions, thoughts, memories.

I guess I must be integrated. It happened during this morning's session. Gerry had me/us lie on the couch and do the exercise. He said it seemed to have brought the integration process along this far, so we ought to keep using it. As soon as I started the exercise, I got in touch with feelings of terror. I remembered how afraid I'd been all during my childhood, how terrified I had been of my mother. Every moment had been a horror. I had never realized how terrorized I had been, even though I knew it was an awful childhood. By the time I stopped crying something had happened—I knew I was really Mildred and Jennifer—that we were really one in some essential, final way. I said to Gerry, "I'm really Jennifer and Mildred. I really am this time."

Afterward he told me about an article he'd read reporting on recent research on multiple personality disorder. He said there were three stages of integration. The first was "co-consciousness," when the core personality knows about the alter personalities and they're all conscious of one another, but the various personalities still think of themselves as separate people. In the second stage, the personalities stop thinking of themselves as separate people and acknowledge that they're all aspects of the same person—they begin to coordinate their activities together. In the final stage of integration the personalities merge as one cohesive whole and no longer think of themselves as separate.

According to Gerry, this whole process can take years. He also found out that the famous Sybil *wasn't* completely integrated when she left her therapist. The hypnotic transference wore off, he said, and she went back to being a multiple personality—although she had achieved co-consciousness. I understand she's now working as an art therapist somewhere in the East. I was thinking—and I told Gerry this—I'd like to meet her.

Gerry was so funny after I did the exercise and kept staring at me with this amazed expression. "I can't believe how different you look. You still have Jennifer's vulnerability but you also have an aura of strength and calm." Nice. On my way home I received more positive feedback, this time from an old friend, a woman I used to know when I was dancing. She couldn't get over how well I looked, and kept saying, "You look wonderful! You look really good!" She seemed terribly surprised that I could look so good. But then, she was always sort of jealous of my relationship with Henrietta.

However, all this positive feedback is confusing. On the one hand it's exhilarating, but on the other it's infuriating. It makes me all the more angry at my parents for terrorizing me. So much time has been wasted because of them—in fact I feel as if I've been walking around in a straitjacket all these years, using only the tiniest part of my potential.

JESS, AUGUST 20

OR THE first time in my life I'm REALLY in love! I never thought I'd feel that particular emotion, not me, not happy-go-lucky Jess. Love 'em and leave 'em, that's my motto.

I told Gerry I loved him today. He gave me one of his typically stern, psychoanalyst looks and asked me how it felt. I said it felt GREAT. He asked where it felt great. I said it felt GREAT all THROUGH my body! In my toes! In my eyelashes! In my earlobes! Love was OOZING out of all my pores! I did the old eye-blink routine that always drives men wild. He made another stern psychoanalyst face.

He's SO serious. I love to tease him almost more than anybody in the world. I've been teasing him about integration. He keeps wanting me to say I am Jennifer, and I keep asking why I'd EVER want to say I was Jennifer when I was happy to be myself. Then I told him to forget integration, just forget it, and fly to Hawaii with me for the weekend. He gave me another stern look.

He's SO gullible sometimes. He actually thought I MEANT it and started to lecture me on how I had already used up THREE credit cards on jaunts to Hawaii, Rio and Paris. (Actually, it was four, counting one from Macy's, but fortunately I hadn't told him about that one or he'd have lectured me much MUCH more.)

However, I lied and said I had some money saved (this month's S.S.D. check, ha ha). "What time do you finish work on Friday?" I said. "How about if I come by for you in a taxi and we head straight for the airport?

We'll take the first plane we can get to Hawaii. Wouldn't that be NEAT?"

"I have to do my laundry this weekend," he said. He's VERY practical.

"We'll buy whatever clothes we need when we get there. Haven't you ever done anything extravagant before?"

"Not really."

"Oh, it's fun. You ought to try it. I've done it LOTS of times. In fact, the last time I went to Hawaii I didn't even have a suitcase. It was incredible. It's a fantastic feeling to just take off on a plane one night after work, on an impulse, and wind up in Hawaii the next morning, like you just stepped out of a subway in Brooklyn, only instead of Brighton Beach you've got Waikiki Beach and beautiful palm trees and the most INCREDIBLE flowers in the world. Come on, be a good sport!" I flashed my most winning smile, a smile that generally makes men want to KILL for me. "Want to go?"

"I don't think so."

"Oh, well. Some other time."

"What do you think about what's been happening with Jennifer and Mildred?" he asked.

"I knew you were going to ask that."

"Wouldn't you like to be part of the team?"

"I'm not a team player. I'm a soloist."

"Will you answer one question?"

"There he goes with the questions again."

"Seriously, how do you feel about Jennifer? Do you like her?"

"I don't like to be bored."

"You don't seem to have much compassion for her."

"Should I?"

"Yes. Compassion and love."

"I certainly don't LOVE her."

"How about yourself? Do you love yourself?"

"Myself? Yes. Me, I love!" I winked at him.

"Jennifer IS yourself," he said. Then he got on his integration bandwagon. "Jennifer's a part of you, so it would be best if you start learning how to love her. You're Jennifer's id," he said. "You represent her sexual outrage at her father. You and Jennifer and Mildred are going to be one soon. You need them."

I let him go on for a while, and then I said, "I'll make a deal. I'll cooperate with you if you'll go to Hawaii this weekend."

"No deals."

I let out a moan. "You know, you're the first man who's ever turned me down."

"See you Monday," he said.

"Maybe. If you're lucky!"

I don't know if I'll be back next Monday or not. I believe in living for the moment. Who knows WHERE I'll be on Monday. I might go to Hawaii by myself.

I'll probably be back, though. Maybe after we're all integrated . . . who knows? He's so cute and so ETHI-CAL he makes me almost want to do ANYTHING for him. Well, almost anything! To tell you the truth, I DO feel a tad lonely. It DEFINITELY has not been as much fun since Jennifer and Mildred have merged.

JESS/JENNIFER/MILDRED,
AUGUST 23

MONDAY, I think . . .
I was so afraid of integration, so afraid that I (the Jess part of me) wouldn't be happy anymore. In fact, the primary question I wanted to ask Gerry when I went for my appointment today was, would I still be happy. He gave me/us one of his patented lectures.

"You'll be happy in a different way. Since you'll now be aware of Jennifer's and Mildred's feelings and identify them as your own, you'll be happy in a more grounded way. You'll feel a lot of new emotions. You can't really experience the full depth of love and joy unless you also experience the full range of sadness and even hate. In a way love and hate are the same thing, like water can be hot or cold but it's always water. The opposite of love isn't hate, it's apathy—the absence of any feeling. Don't be afraid of feeling your hate, Jess. You're not really as happy as you think you are, and the sooner you realize that, the more contented you'll be. Your compulsive drive for happiness is really a doomed attempt to spite your father and, on another level, a search for the Good Daddy who will accept your sexuality and give you contentment."

When he'd finished his lecture I began to cry. Me, Jess, crying? It was a first. But actually I'd already begun to feel Jennifer's sadness last night. Now I sat on the couch crying. I don't know what made me start to cry—I suppose something he said about my compulsive search for happiness struck home. I realized how rejected I always felt by my father. I thought I had a thick skin and it didn't hurt me when he called me names like "whore" and "slut," but it did, it really did. "I wanted his love so much . . . I was willing to do ANYTHING for his love," I said. I sat on his couch for about twenty minutes crying and carrying on about my father and other things I hadn't thought about for years, including the time he'd caught me in the basement with Hank, the neighborhood boy. I wanted to kill him then. I really wanted to kill the bastard.

I cried until the session was almost over, then sat up and said, "That's all the crying I have in me for that man."

"Are you Jennifer now?" Gerry asked.

"Yes, I'm Jennifer . . . and I'm Mildred . . . and I'm Jess." I felt so strange. One minute there was a rush of joy, then of fear, then of sadness. "I feel as though I've just awakened from a trance," I said.

"In a way, you have. Up to now you've been sleep-walking."

"Oh, God. This is weird."

"I think it's great. Now three of my favorite female personalities are combined into one."

"Better watch out," I said. "Margaret will be jealous."

"That's all right. She's next."

Gerry said I'd feel more contented when I merged. He was right about that, I do feel more contented. But I also experience a wider range of emotions and thoughts, and that's sort of disconcerting. Just before I sat down to write this I had a feeling of doom like you wouldn't believe. Then there was a rush of elation that was frightening. I feel as if I'm on an emotional rollercoaster. But it's fine, it's really fine. At least I've got to keep telling myself that.

MARGARET, AUGUST 25

I SAID I didn't want to come in for the session but he insisted. I told him I had a respiratory infection and besides, I didn't need therapy. But he told me to come in anyway. He has a certain charm, and he's used it to beguile Jennifer, Mildred and Jess. Now he thinks he can charm me. He's just like every other man I've ever met. They all think they're superior, that they have a natural right to order women around.

"Come in anyway," he says, when I told him I had the respiratory infection. "Sometimes when you're feeling sick you have your best therapy session." I told him that was bullshit but he wouldn't let it go.

I don't know why I went in for the therapy session. I should have said no. As soon as I walked in the door I knew it wasn't going to work. I wasn't really into it. For one thing, I don't like being in a room with a man. You never know what they'll do. They think all women are pieces of meat for them to take advantage of. I'll kill any man who tries to lay a hand on me. Including Gerry. I'm grateful that he's helped Jennifer, but that doesn't give him any rights. I'm not scared of any man.

But he acted like he wasn't interested in me, physically. Men always act like that. I don't trust it. He acted like all he was interested in was integrating me.

"What's been happening?" he says to me when I sat down.

"I have a respiratory infection." I stared at him until he looked away. I can stare down any man.

"How've you been feeling about integration?" he asks me.

"I don't have any feelings about it one way or another," I tell him.

"What do you think about what's been happening to Jennifer, Mildred and Jess?" he asks.

"That's their business," I say.

Then he says, "Have you been aware of Jennifer's feelings inside you?"

I lied and said, "Not at all." Actually I'd been feeling strange lately, but I wasn't going to tell him that.

Then he starts giving orders. He wanted me to lie on the couch. I told him no. He said, "Margaret, lie on the couch." I said no. But he's just like my father. Once he gets something in his head, he won't let it go. I finally got on the couch to appease him. I knew I wasn't going to do anything.

Then he asked me to stamp my feet. He wanted me to stamp my feet and hit and scream, like Jennifer. No way. "I've got an upper respiratory infection and you want me to scream? Forget it," I told him.

"All right," he says in his bossy, therapy voice. "That's okay," he says. "Tell me this, are you in touch with any feelings?" He was sitting on a chair next to me. He was too close. He was practically on top of me. He was making me nervous and pissed. And they *always*, say that crap about being in touch with your feelings.

"I don't know," I say. "I don't know what I *feel*."

Then he wants to know, "Are you angry?"

"I'm always angry," I tell him.

"Do you feel angry at me?" he asks.

"I don't feel *anything* about you," I lied.

Then he starts giving orders again. "Say 'I don't want to feel anything about you, Gerry,' " he tells me.

"Why should I say that?" I say to him. I looked at him and tried to stare him down. But he wouldn't look away.

"Just say it," he says.

To humor him, I say 'I don't want to feel anything for you, Gerry."

"How does that feel?" he wants to know.

I shrugged my shoulders.

"Say 'I don't want to need you, Gerry,' " he tells me.

"I don't want to need you, Gerry," I say.

"How does that feel?" he asks.

"I don't feel anything," I lied. Actually, I could feel something but I didn't want to let on. I didn't know why I was doing any of this. I felt like running out the door. I don't know why I stayed.

Then he says, "Say 'I don't want to feel scared like Jennifer.' "

"I don't want to say that," I told him.

"Say it," he says.

"Why?"

"Say it," he says again.

"I don't want to feel scared like Jennifer," I say.

"Say 'I *am* Jennifer,' " he says.

"I *am* Jennifer," I repeated after him. I could feel my body shaking and my voice getting foggy. I really wanted to run for the door.

"Do you really feel you're Jennifer?" he asks.

"In fact, yes," I finally admitted. "But not really."

"What does that mean?" he wants to know.

"Intellectually, as you like to say, I can see that I'm Jennifer, but in my gut I don't think I am," I tell him.

"Don't you think it's curious that Mildred and Jess are Jennifer, but you aren't?" he says in his arrogant, masculine way.

"I don't know," I say, and I sit up. "Is it almost time?" I ask him.

"We have a few more minutes," he says, and looks at me like he thought he was strong and sexy. "What are you feeling about me right now?"

"That you're sitting too close," I tell him.

"What does that make you feel?" he wants to know.

"Uncomfortable," I say.

"Uncomfortable? How?" he wants to know.

"Scared," I tell him.

"Of what?" he persists.

"I don't know," I say.

"How about 'I don't want to know,' " he says.

"I *do* want to know," I corrected him. "I just don't want to say."

"Say it," he orders me.

Now I'm pissed again. I want to get out of there. He's practically on top of me again.

"All right, I'll tell you," I say. "But first you have to sit over there." I pointed to the other chair.

He moved away. "Now, tell me."

"Promise you won't laugh?" I say.

"I promise," he says.

"I felt scared of my sexual feelings," I told him.

"Wonderful," he says, and he's got this big grin on his face. "That means you're close to integration." He was pleased with himself. With his male ego, he probably took credit for everything.

It was nearly time to go. He looked at his watch, and then he asks me, "Tell me, did you really feel all the things you've said?"

"I felt all of them," I told him. I don't know why I told him that. I don't need to prove anything to him. But it was like there was another part of me that I hadn't felt before, that wanted to prove something. It was making me sick.

He looked so smug I wanted to kill him. But, for the first time in my life, I felt embarrassed. I never feel embarrassed about anything, but I did then. I felt angry and embarrassed. I think if I'd had a gun I would have shot him. I really would have.

Before I left I told him, "I don't trust you. I don't trust your niceness."

"You're afraid to let in my positive feelings," he said.
"You're full of crap," I told him.

NOW I'M lying in bed and my respiratory infection is worse than ever, thanks to him. He claims this infection is a sign that my defenses are breaking down, that it's a "somatization of my feelings." I say that's bullshit. All I know is I'm tired of being sick. There are things to do around here, and if I don't do them, nobody will. The laundry needs to be done, the rent has to be paid, and I'll probably have to get a job soon.

I don't think I'm going to show up for Friday's appointment. To hell with him.

JENNIFER/MILDRED/JESS/ MARGARET, AUGUST 27

IT SEEMS I've surrendered and become one with Jennifer. I suppose it was inevitable.

I went to today's therapy session thinking I was going to tell Gerry off. I went in as Margaret feeling really pissed at him. I didn't want any bossy male prick coming close to me.

"I'm pissed," I told him when I arrived. I went and sat down on the sofa and tried to stare him down.

"Why are you pissed?" he asked.

"I've been pissed since Wednesday."

"How come?"

I sat with my arms folded and my legs crossed because I didn't want to be there. I really hated him and all his questions, but I also felt afraid of him for the first time.

"I still don't trust you," I said.

"What don't you trust?"

"I'm reading this spy novel," I said. "Sometimes I feel like a spy. The protagonist in this book is very isolated, doesn't trust anybody. I feel like that. He doesn't want anybody to know too much about him. That's how I feel. I think I'm pissed at you because you know too much about me."

"What do I know about you?"

"It's not what you know. It's what you *think* you know. You think you know that I'm not a hard-assed bitch. That I'm really soft inside."

"Are you?"

His questions were making me even more pissed. He

was being so calm and smug, just like a man. "If I were a spy I'd have to shoot you," I said.

He went to his desk, opened a drawer, and pulled out a toy pistol—one of those water guns kids get from variety stores. "Go ahead," he said, handing me the gun. "Shoot me." He sat down and clasped his hands.

I aimed the pistol at him and pretended to shoot him five, six, seven, eight times. I made a clicking sound with my tongue while I was shooting him. He didn't even flinch. I stood up and walked over to him with the gun and held it to his temple and made several more clicking sounds. Then I pointed the gun at his prick and made several more clicking sounds. He still didn't flinch.

"That's it," I said, tossing the gun on the desk. "You're dead."

"Is that what you really want? To kill me?" He was actually smiling.

"That's right," I said. "I guess." When I sat back down, I felt a little sad. Sad and disgusted.

"Is that really what you want? Is it?" he asked again, and his eyes were suddenly angry, as though I'd really shot him. "You know," he said, "*I* feel pissed at *you*. I've been trying to be nice to you, and this is what I get. It doesn't pay to be nice to you."

"What should I do?" I asked. I was feeling sad *and* sick inside. "Tell me what to do."

"I don't care. Do what you want."

"I need some guidance. I feel abandoned."

"If I give you guidance you'll think I'm ordering you around. If I don't I'm abandoning you. You put me into a no-win situation."

"I *want* your guidance now," I said.

"Guide yourself."

"I can't. My head aches too much."

"Give your headache a voice. What would it say?"

"It says, 'I need you, Gerry.'"

He leaned forward in his chair when I said that. Then he said, "Say, 'I'm scared to feel vulnerable.' "

"I'm scared to feel vulnerable," I said, and continued on my own. "I need to feel my vulnerability. I need . . . to integrate with Jennifer. . . ." I cried for a while, and it came into my head, as I cried, how angry I am at both my father and mother, and especially at those black punks who raped Jennifer/me. They're the ones I'd really like to kill. Then, as I cried, all the men who've ever taken advantage of and abandoned Jennifer/me flashed through my head. I wanted to kill them all—my mother, father, those black punks, and all those untrustworthy men. "Fuck them all!" I screamed at one point, and then I didn't feel so angry at them anymore, nor at myself, but just sad about everything. After about twenty minutes I sighed and looked up at Gerry, and I was flooded with all kinds of new sensations. I guess I knew I'd been somehow transformed.

"Are you Jennifer?" he asked, smiling like he meant it.

"Yes."

"You look different," he said, sitting back to look at me. "You look strong."

"I . . . feel strong."

I felt strong and vulnerable at the same time.

I'M NOT Margaret now. I'm Jennifer/Margaret/Mildred/ Jess. We're all writing this together, and it's damn strange. We're fighting among ourselves about what to say. I suppose we're not totally integrated, but at least we've agreed on one thing. . . . that we're all parts of the same person.

JENNY, SEPTEMBER 3

INEVER learned how to write. I mean, I learned a little in school, but not much. I think I'm very smart. But my mum does not think I am smart. But Gerry thinks I am smart. I think he is smart too and nice. He is smarter than my mum.

I feel funny now. I wish Jennifer was here. I wish Jess was here too. I like Jess. She used to play with me a lot. They all went away. I miss them. I used to be able to talk to them. Now I never talk to them.

Gerry called me on the phone. He wants me to come to see him. He says I can play with Dolly. He wants me to do intagrayshun, he says. I mean integration. Mary told me how to spell it. Mary is very smart, but she is not fun. Jess is lots of fun. I really miss her.

Gerry says Jess misses me too. He says if we do integration I can play with Jess. He says Dolly misses me and wants me to play with her too. He says he bought a new dress for Dolly. He says she has been lonely and afraid sitting on his shelf.

I think Gerry is nice for a grown-up. Most grown-ups are not very nice. My mum is not very nice. I should not talk about her that way, but it is true. She does not think I understand things. She says I'm stupid. But I am not stupid. I understand everything. I understand how mean she is. I understand how she lies.

I think I will go to see Gerry tomorrow. I think he is a nice man who wants to help me.

JENNIFER/MILDRED/JESS/
MARGARET/JENNY,
SEPTEMBER 5

GERRY IS SO wonderful! He let me play with Dolly the whole session, and then at the end he presented her to me as a gift. He was so sweet, I started to cry. The Jenny part of me was afraid that if I joined the others I wouldn't be free anymore, and that I'd have to do what they told me to do and wouldn't be able to play any longer. But it's sort of neat to be integrated. I'm full of energy now, and also brimming with all sorts of new information I didn't know I had. There's also a curious kind of sadness that is not terribly pleasant to deal with, but Gerry said I'd feel more alive and I certainly do feel that.

He let me play with Dolly nearly all session and he didn't say a word to me. Then he said, "She's yours, for keeps."

"Really?" I replied. I almost cried right then, but I kept it in. "I'll take good care of her," I said. "My mum said I didn't know how to take care of dolls but I do."

"I think you'll take excellent care of Dolly," he said.

"As soon as I get home I'm going to wash her hair," I said. "It needs a good washing."

Then he started asking me about integration, and would I like to join Jennifer, and the others. I said I didn't know if they wanted me to join them.

He asked me if I knew the story of Snow White. He said he wanted me to pretend to be Snow White sleeping and he would be the prince, and when he kissed me I'd be

Jennifer. Then he told me to sit very still and close my eyes and not to open them again until he said so. He said when I opened them I'd be Jennifer.

"Will you still be my Good Daddy afterwards?" I asked.

He said, "Sure."

So I went on the couch and shut my eyes real tight, and then I felt him kiss me on the cheek. When I opened my eyes I felt very sad and was about to cry, but I stopped myself. Then I felt myself sort of changing inside, and felt a tremendous surge of energy.

"Are you Jennifer?" Gerry asked.

And I said, "Yes."

"Are you Jenny?"

"Yes."

Then he wanted to know how it felt.

It felt wonderful—like waking up on Christmas Day. "I feel great!" I told him. I feel—this is crazy—I feel like doing a somersault." I somersaulted on the couch and then stood on my head. I had the energy of a kid, but the mind of an adult. It was strange for parts of me (Margaret and Mildred) to experience tumbling through the air like that. I never knew I had so much energy.

I CAN'T quite believe that all this is happening to me. I must be dreaming. It's really unbelievable. Every day brings new surprises and new revelations. Integration isn't bad AT ALL!

JENNIFER/MILDRED/JESS/
MARGARET/JENNY,
LATER THAT NIGHT

I THINK Gerry's miffed, and I really can't blame him. He's done so much for me/us, and I think he's feeling drained. He didn't say anything about it when he came over tonight, but I could tell. Perhaps I/we shouldn't have called him, but it seemed unavoidable.

When I left his office today I knew there was something wrong. The Jennifer part of me felt like a volcano again that was about to explode. After sundown I started feeling terribly frightened, and I felt as though I were six years old again, and I started remembering things that happened then and it seemed as though they were happening in the present. Does that make sense? I've never been so scared in my life. I covered myself with a blanket and the Jenny part of myself started sucking her thumb. I sat on my sofa, covered with the blanket, and hoped it would all go away, but of course it didn't. That's when I called Gerry.

"I'm scared," I told him. "It's starting to happen now."

He just answered "I'd better come over," and hung up.

I WAS still on the sofa with the blanket over my head when he got here. He looked annoyed at me. I guess for making him come over.

"What's happening?" he said.

I took my thumb out of my mouth and told him, "I'm scared."

He looked at me as if he thought I was crazy, and maybe I was. I felt paralyzed sitting under the blanket, staring into space and sucking my thumb. He seemed impatient with me. "Keep saying that," he told me. "Keep saying, 'I'm scared.'"

"I'm scared," I said again. "I'm scared. I'm scared. I'm scared." All at once I clamped both my hands over my face, because I could feel the explosion coming. Then I was crying and crying, and I remembered being in bed with my mother, and it seemed as though it was happening right now, and I kept crying out, "Please don't hurt me, Mummy. Please. Please don't hurt me. . . ." I cried a long, long time, and I also remembered my mother taking my hand once and placing it on the oven door because I'd said something sarcastic to her—as Jenny. I still have a scar on the side of my hand from that burn. And I also remembered the time I wouldn't eat my stew and she dropped the whole bowl of stew on my head. And later Daddy came home when I was taking a bath and he burst right into the bathroom and pulled off his belt and whipped me. I was so scared, I pooped in the tub. Then he got even angrier and whipped me again for pooping in the tub. I didn't want to be there, didn't want to be in the bathroom with him—I wanted to run to the closet and hide—but I couldn't. I was so scared all the time in those days, so awfully scared all the time. It was so horrible.

"It's all right, it's over now," Gerry said when I stopped crying and gathered myself together.

"They were really mean people," I said. "I never want to see them again."

Gerry stayed a few minutes to make sure I was okay. He said he thought he might have rushed things during our session earlier today, and you couldn't rush the process of integration. He thought we hadn't allowed these feelings to come out in the office, and that's why they had erupted now. I agreed. He said he thought the worst was over and I said I sure *hoped* so.

After he left I felt guilty for calling him, but I couldn't help it. I was so scared. I hope he's not too annoyed with me.

JENNIFER, ET AL.,
SEPTEMBER 7

I WAS right about Gerry, he was angry at me. But I didn't notice it at first because I was too excited, full of this mixture of new feelings and memories that had rushed through my body since the other night.

I went to my session today wearing red shorts and a pink polka dot halter that belonged to the Jenny part of me, but Gerry hardly seemed to notice. I was so excited I couldn't wait to tell Gerry about the new pattern I'd observed, which happens each time a new personality joins "the group." It's like there's a period of a day or so following the initial integration in which the new personality is still not quite assimilated, a period of digestion. Memories have to be exchanged, activities coordinated, and feelings sorted out. Additionally, for a while the new personality isn't quite accepted by "the group," and also for a while the new personality dominates the total character structure, sort of like when you add a new chemical to a mixture and it fizzes for a while until the new chemical breaks down. For instance, all day I've wanted to play with Dolly and I've also had this incredible urge for vanilla ice cream. And when I had lunch at Kentucky Fried Chicken, I discovered myself licking my fingers after I had eaten. An older woman stared at me and I smiled like a kid at her.

But when I told all this to Gerry he didn't seem excited about it. He wasn't the same Gerry. And then I remembered how annoyed he had looked when I called him the other night, and so I finally asked him, "Is something wrong?"

At first he tried to avoid me. "Why do you ask?"

"You have a look on your face. It's the same look you had on your face the other night."

"What kind of look is it?"

"You look annoyed."

"Why would I be annoyed?"

"Because I made you come over to my house. And I *do* feel guilty about that. I felt guilty about it as soon as you left. I'm sorry, I know I must be very difficult to work with. I promise I'll pay you for all the sessions you've done without charge. You have my word on that." He didn't speak for several moments and I said, "You *are* angry, aren't you? Please tell me if you are."

"Maybe your therapy has been a little exhausting for me. But I'll deal with that. That's not your concern. Right now the most important thing is to get you completely integrated."

"But it *is* my concern," I protested. "I don't want to be a bother."

"You're not a being a bother, you're being a patient."

"But a bothersome patient."

"All right, suppose we say you *are* a bother. What would that mean to you?"

"I'd be afraid you'd get tired of me and leave me."

"I see. So if you perceive me as having a look of annoyance or anger on my face, you feel afraid I'm going to abandon you the way so many others have throughout your life."

"Yes."

"That's the transference," he said. "You're transferring your mother onto me. You're afraid I'm going to begin to see you as no good, and that I'll turn on you the way she did."

HE KEPT reassuring me but I'm not sure I feel reassured. I'm having doubts about whether integration is such a good idea. Also, I'm afraid that I've become too dependent on him. Maybe it's transference, like he says, but I do feel very frightened that he's going to get tired of me and, yes, leave me. This is my pattern and I know it's my pattern, but knowing about it doesn't seem to help me control it.

TOM, SEPTEMBER 14

IF GERRY keeps pushing it I might just decide to smash his face in. He kept wanting me to come to his office but I didn't want to. I'm not interested, period. The only reason I decided to show up is because he bribed me. He found out from the women that I've always wanted a Swiss pocket knife. So he got me one, but I had to go to his office to pick it up.

I knew what to expect when I got there, and I was right. He kept running off at the mouth about integration. He didn't know it but I'd already made up my mind what I was going to do. I was just going to take the knife, listen to what he had to say and get out.

Naturally, he wanted to know how I felt about Jennifer's integration. I told him I thought it was great. I knew that would surprise him. He wanted to know why. I said because now all the women were off my back. He asked if I felt lonely and I said no. Then he wondered if I'd ever thought I might be better off integrated with Jennifer. Again I said the answer was no, period. That threw him off.

Then he started telling me I wasn't a boy. He said, if I was a boy, where was my cock? *That* really pissed me off. I felt like hauling off and smashing him, but I just said it was there, he shouldn't worry about it. But he kept it up. Where was my cock, like he wanted me to prove it or something. So I told him I was deformed. He didn't know what I meant so I told him about my operation. The women didn't want a cock so I had an operation to have it put inside my thigh. He didn't buy that. He claimed the operation I was talking about was an operation to remove

Jennifer's cyst. I said, that's what she thinks. He kept saying I was imagining things.

I really almost smashed him right then and there. Finally, he told me I should check to see what was between my legs, I'd find a vagina. I told him that wasn't mine, it was theirs. Then he warned me that sooner or later I'd have to accept that I'm a woman.

Accept that I'm a woman? I'd die first. That really got me. That really did. I gave him a big smile and asked him how he'd like to be a woman. Why not, he wanted to know. What's wrong with women. I saw through him. Women are dumb, I told him. He wanted to know where I got this information. From my father, I said. He reminded me that I hated my father's guts. By then he was starting to bore me and I told him so. Then I stood up and walked out the door. The asshole followed me to the waiting room. I said I didn't want to talk about it anymore, and I thanked him for the knife. I said I had to go. But he kept standing there blabbering away and wouldn't let me go.

He reminded me that I'd promised to come for three sessions if he gave me the knife. I said I didn't remember promising that. He said he'd see me on Wednesday. I said I'd think about it. I couldn't give him any guarantee. I'll think about it, I told him, period.

That was this morning. I'm still thinking about it. But not very much. Frankly, there are more important things on my mind than him. Much more important things.

JENNIFER, ET AL.,
SEPTEMBER 16

I T HAPPENED today—the Tom part of me finally "surrendered" to integration. Sort of. He's agreed to be part of "the group," but he's not ready yet to give up his masculine identity. I think that will still take some time.

I'm not quite sure why the Tom part of me decided to come in today, because I was sure I wasn't coming in. But at the last minute I walked out of the house. It was as if some magnetic force were drawing me to Gerry's office. When I arrived he had already planned an exercise for me.

"Would you like to play a game?" he asked.

"What kind of game?"

"You said you wanted to beat up your father."

"That's right."

He took a big stuffed pillow out of a closet and tossed it onto the floor. "This is your father."

"You want me to pretend that's my father?"

"That's right."

I looked at the pillow and smiled. "I don't want to pretend. I *really* want to beat him up. And I'm going to someday."

He asked me what was more important, getting rid of my anger at my father or getting rid of my father. I had to admit, it was a good point. But I was convinced it would be a phony exercise so I just sat there looking at the pillow. To me it was just a pillow.

Then he said, "All right, if you don't want to beat him up, I'll do it for you," and he started kicking the pillow around the room and swearing at it. I knew he was trying to provoke me, and he succeeded. I kept thinking that he wasn't angry enough, not the way I was angry. He wasn't doing anything at all to that pillow.

"Stand aside," I said. I was so sore at him for making me do the stupid exercise I decided to destroy his pillow. I wasn't thinking about my father at all. But then as I started hitting and kicking the pillow I saw his face, and the anger started gushing out of me. "That's for fucking my mother in front of me!" I heard myself suddenly yelling, kicking him in the balls. "And that's for hitting and kicking me in the head!" I kicked and kicked at the pillow, then picked it up and threw it to the floor and stamped on it. I stamped on his face until it was a bloody mess. Finally I was exhausted. "He's dead!" I said, and slunk into a chair.

"Why did you want to kill him?"

I didn't know how he could ask such a dumb question. It really irritated me. "*Why?*" I said. "Why? Because I hate his guts, that's why. He thinks he's so smart, a big shot, and he's not! He's nothing but an asshole, a hypocritical asshole! I don't need a reason, I just hate his guts, O.K.? I hate his guts!" My body was shaking by then and my throat was getting tight and I felt things inside me I'd never felt before—I mean, the Tom part of me felt the other parts, especially Jennifer's depression, and heard voices, and he panicked. He stood up, his hands on his temples, and called out, "Oh, God, tell me I'm not going crazy, tell me I'm not going out of my mind—"

"You're not going crazy," Gerry said.

"Then what's happening?"

"You're not crazy. You've just gotten in touch with the other parts of yourself!"

"Oh, God. This is really insane."

Then I/we couldn't hold it in anymore, and started crying. The Tom part of me thought it was all very mushy to cry like that, but there was nothing to do about it. I/he leaned against the wall, embarrassed to be crying, but the embarrassment soon withered and I cried uninhibitedly. Then, while the Tom part was crying, he could suddenly hear the voices of Jennifer and Mildred and Jess and Margaret and Jenny, all talking to him at once, all telling him to say "I'm Jennifer."

I turned from the wall and looked up at Gerry. We were standing face to face.

He asked, "Are you Jennifer?"

"Yes, I'm Jennifer," the Tom part reluctantly said.

"And are you Tom?"

"Yes," the rest of us said. "I'm Tom. And I'm Jennifer."

There was a new, invigorating feeling of physical strength at that moment. What a *feeling!* It was sort of like it had been when "the group" had been infused with Jenny's youthful energy. Now we'd gotten a "shot" of Tom's physical power, and it was amazing. I felt as though I could have gone twelve rounds with Mike Tyson.

MARY, SEPTEMBER 18

I AM Mary. But who am I? I'm the last stronghold. The equilibrium of our system has been upset five times now. I no longer feel a part of a system or a family. I feel all alone. And for the first time I feel unsure of myself, depressed. What does *that* mean?

I am not one for expressing myself. I am much better at observing and listening to others. I am a person who is externally oriented. I don't feel inside too much. I have tried to leave. It is not possible. I wanted to go back to England, I cannot. Must I accept myself as part of the others? Is this truly what it has come to? Is there no other alternative?

I feel trapped. I feel that I am being forced to give up myself, my identity. Who is this man who has had such a tremendous impact on our lives? How has it been allowed that a stranger has so much power and control? Why have all of us thrown ourselves into his arms?

Still, if the inevitable is that I must surrender, give up myself into the others . . . It is said, parting is such sweet sorrow. Well, joining also requires a parting. If some do not understand, just call it Zen.

MARY, JENNIFER, ET AL.,
SEPTEMBER 21

INTEGRATION IS not really as frightening as I imagined. And it happened quite easily.

"It seems that integration is, as you put it, inevitable," I said to Gerry. "But I must confess I have some qualms about it."

"Yes?" He sat back in his imitation leather chair. I dislike anything fake but said nothing to him out of politeness. "What are your qualms?" he asked.

"As I wrote in the diary, I feel I am the last stronghold. If I surrender to you, we are completely yours."

"You see this as something you're doing for me rather than for yourself?"

"Yes, it seems so. Although I suppose that is not really it. I have always been a loner. I do not know if I would blend in with the others. And I know that Jennifer is not particularly keen about having me join her. And there is a fear on her part that after we are completely integrated you won't like her anymore. The challenge, so to speak, will be over."

"I think these qualms are well taken," he said. "What could I say to relieve them?"

"I am not sure there is anything you could say."

"So even if I tried to convince you that you're doing this for yourself and not me, or to persuade you that Jennifer really wants you, or to assure you that I'll still like Jennifer after she's integrated, you wouldn't necessarily be reassured by it."

"Correct."

"In that case, perhaps we should just get on with it, since you've said you think integration is inevitable anyway."

"Perhaps so."

"Good." He flashed the boyish grin that the Jess part of me always finds so disarming.

"What should I do?" I asked with some resignation.

"I think you probably know."

"Should I say 'I'm Jennifer'?"

"Good idea."

"I am not certain I am Jennifer."

"Say it anyway."

"I'm Jennifer."

"How was it?"

"It felt unsettling."

"Say it again."

The Mary part of me paused for a moment, suspicious of Gerry but wanting to cooperate. She said it again, and then I/we felt myself stiffen up. It was incredible how *stiff* I was. Then things gradually loosened up and I felt a stream of emotions rush through me.

"Mary is a very tense lady," I told Gerry. "Correction: Mary *was* a very tense lady."

JENNIFER, ET AL.,
SEPTEMBER 23

I NTEGRATION (OR, as Gerry calls it, co-consciousness) is wonderful!

I feel very strong and secure inside. For the first time in my life I think I really know myself. I've spent twenty-nine years deluding myself, and I don't need to anymore. And I have this feeling that whatever comes along I've already been through the worst and survived. No—better than that—I've gotten over it! I haven't felt pessimistic in weeks, at least not for any long period of time. I always used to feel doom hanging over me, even when I was dancing for Apple, but not any longer. I feel optimistic, lucky to be where I am. I'm even hopeful I'll dance again, and that this time I'll be able to handle the pressures that go with it. Oh, I still have moments of real doubt, when I wonder when the rug will be pulled out from under me. But not nearly as many of these times as I used to.

I'm still sort of in flux, but it's okay. No, I'm *not* completely integrated yet. It's only the first step, the co-consciousness stage. Listen, I can still hear the voices of the others in my head, and I still feel myself being one or another personality at different times. Right this minute, for example, I'm aware of being mostly Mildred, with everybody else sort of looking on. Maybe that's because the Mildred part of me is by far the best writer. There are also times when I plain forget *which* I am, when I seem to become a mixture of some or all—a really combined personality. It's fascinating how it all works. Sometimes I try to stand outside myself and see me/us from Gerry's point of view. It's all too fantastic for words. Literally.

Gerry tells me I've never looked so alive and healthy. I feel that way too. Sometimes it seems as if I've come back from the dead.

And I don't think I'll be having any more of these blackouts! I can't quite believe it yet. I asked Gerry today if he thought I would.

"I can't say for sure, but I'd guess you won't have any more blackouts," he said. "There have been cases where MPDs have had relapses, but usually these are cases where only hypnosis was used to bring on integration, where there wasn't enough working through, or emotional reconstruction."

"You mean all that crying I did is going to pay off?"

"Yes, that and the talking about and releasing of traumatic memories and feelings."

"Then I'm cured?"

"I don't like that word."

"Finished?"

"What do you think? Do you feel finished?"

"No, not really."

"How much longer do you think you'll need to be in therapy?" he asked.

"Sometimes," I told him, "I think I could spend the rest of my life in therapy."

He nodded. I didn't know whether he agreed or not.

Which brings me to the one thing that's been concerning me lately—Gerry's being irritable and distracted. It first happened during Jenny's integration, when I called him to come to my apartment. Although, now that I think of it, there were probably signs of it before that. I have this feeling he's moving away from me somehow. I want to say it's all just my imagination. I also worry that now that I've become integrated he'll lose interest in me.

He said something about me doing classical psychoanalysis, and I wasn't sure how he meant it. "When you first came to me classical psychoanalysis wouldn't have worked," he said. "You needed something more intense and active. Now you've gotten over your crisis and are ready for a more long-term reconstructive analysis. I think you'll be a terrific psychoanalytic patient." What troubled me about him saying that is he didn't include himself in the picture. Was he thinking of classical analysis with himself, or somebody else?

He's the best therapist I've ever had. I would really hate to lose him.

But except for this nagging worry, which I'd probably feel about any therapist, things have been going just fine, thank you. And I have the feeling that no matter what happens now, I'll land on my feet. I've sure never felt *that* way before. I can't tell you how good that feels. I can't describe in words how relieved that makes me feel.

IV

TERMINATION

A VISIT TO MY SUPERVISOR

EVERY THERAPEUTIC relationship is a power struggle. In one way or another, at some point or another, the patient attempts to defeat the therapist. Sometimes this is done in an obvious way, such as by trying to outsmart or put down the therapist. Sometimes it's done in a less obvious way, as when a patient ostensibly does everything the therapist asks (while holding back real feelings) in order to lure the therapist into developing a special narcissistic relationship. If the patient wins the power struggle, the therapy is over. Deep down, all patients are searching for a therapist who will not allow defeat, who will prove strong enough to handle any of their neurotic, narcissistic or psychotic behaviors. Only when the therapist has proved this can analysis truly begin.

Jennifer and I never got to this stage. I was not strong enough at that point to handle her. And so things got muddled. I began to have extremely ambivalent feelings about her. Sometimes she was my dream woman come true; sometimes she was a demanding, exhausting creature from the Black Lagoon from whom I needed to flee for my life.

I was torn by countertransference. I would spend days fantasizing about her. I could see myself fulfilling all her longings to be saved by a Good Daddy, and how she would heap gratitude on me, the deepest kind of appreciation born out of her bitterest years of early childhood loneliness. I would actually imagine us getting married (I pictured the wedding at some country church) and buying a house with a few acres of land, happy in our splendid isolation from the world. As I saw it then, I could continue to exert a healthy influence on her if we were married, and soon she would be totally integrated. Or perhaps she would keep her personalities and that would be fine, too, like having a harem, a secret harem. It could be quite fascinating, I thought.

On the other hand, I was completely repulsed by these fantasies and tried to stop myself from having them. I was in torment over them. I was in torment over her. I did not know if they were really my fantasies or the ones *she* had induced in me. I was confused, exhausted and just wanted out. In fact, I had lost my sense of self and had become involved in a symbiotic relationship with her that replicated the one she had had with her mother.

Caught between the poles of longing and fear, not able to sustain a distinction between the transference and the real relationship, I went for clarification from my former supervisor. Dr. Richards had been my case-control supervisor at the institute I had graduated from. He was a short man with thinning hair whose cheeks always seemed rosy and whose large brown eyes looked larger as they peered knowingly and, I thought, a bit cynically through his brown-rimmed glasses.

"I've never had a multiple myself," he said after I had briefed him about the problem. "She sounds fascinating."

"She is."

"And you think you want to marry her?"

"Sometimes. I don't know what to do."

"So why don't you marry her?"

"I'm not sure I'd be doing it for the right reasons. And I'm not sure it would be the best thing for her therapeutically."

"What would be the right reasons for marrying her?"

"If I had decided in a cool and rational way that she was the right person for me, and I was the right person for her, that would be the right reason. But under the circumstances I don't think I can make that kind of cool, rational decision." I felt suddenly hopeful. "Why are you asking? Are you saying I *should* marry her?"

"No, I'm not. I'm just trying to explore your feelings. What are you feeling?" He looked at me with eyes magnified by his glasses.

"Confused. Mixed up. Sometimes I want to run into her arms and live happily ever after. Sometimes I want to run from her like she was the plague. Have you ever felt this way? Have you ever thought seriously about marrying a patient, or having an affair with one? Have you ever had such mixed feelings?"

"Sure, all therapists have these kinds of feelings, particularly in the beginning. Some even act them out. Reich married a patient. Jung had affairs with patients, and there were rumors about Ferenczi. Margaret Mahler had an affair with her training analyst. Fritz Perls slept with hundreds of students. I have a patient right now I'd love to marry and run off with, a beautiful young philosophy student."

"Why don't you?"

"Well, for one thing, my wife wouldn't be too crazy about the idea, and I'd kind of like to keep her." The supervisor pushed his glasses up on his nose and blinked sarcastically at me, making me laugh. "For another thing, I realize that these are the feelings that are being induced in me by this particular patient. They're not my real feelings."

"Don't you ever get emotional about patients?"

"Not the way you mean. I think of them once in a while but not in an emotional way. You know what Freud said, don't you?"

"What did he say?"

"A therapist should be abstinent. He shouldn't get involved with his patients. He stays detached so that he can perform the therapy as cleanly and calmly as possible. He believed therapists should maintain a firm boundary with patients."

"But what if you *love* a patient? What if a patient happens to be just the right woman for you? Is it always transference? Isn't it ever real? What's real, anyway?" I was getting upset.

"I hear you" was all Dr. Richards said, and then he waited.

"So what should I do?"

"What would you like to do?"

"As I said, sometimes I think I want to marry her, and sometimes I want to escape from her."

"What do you think it would be like, marrying her?"

"I think it might be great."

"What happens when she finds out you're just a human being with your own problems, your own fears, your own anger at women. What happens when she needs you to continue to play the role of the omniscient and omnipotent therapist, and you begin feeling more and more drained from it? What happens if she gets suicidal again or develops a transference psychosis toward you? As a therapist you can maintain some distance, but as a husband you'll be even more emotionally involved with her."

I nodded sadly. "These are the hard questions I've been reluctant to ask myself."

"Why?"

"Because I feel trapped. From the beginning she kept telling me how other therapists abandoned her, and how she was afraid to depend on me, on anybody, because they always left her. I don't want to be like everybody else."

"How many therapists has she had?"

"About three or four, I think. All of them male. She's recreating a pattern that goes back to her relationship with her father."

"Maybe she'd work better with a woman."

"I thought of that. Except she had a terrible relationship with her mother too, and would probably have just as much trouble with a woman therapist. So. What do you think I should do?"

"You really want me to tell you?"

"Yes, I really do."

"I think you're overinvolved. If you'd come to me sooner we might have been able to straighten things out. Now, I don't know." The supervisor looked off toward the windows, where the blinds were slightly open, letting in slivers of sun. "Did you ever read Michael Balint?"

"Yes, a while back, for one of my courses."

"Do you remember Balint's discussion about malignant regression?"

"Vaguely."

"Read it again. It might be helpful. I think that might be what's going on here, at least in part. I think you're dealing with a very primitive and intense kind of transference. She's a very difficult patient to handle because she's always throwing so much at you. She's so frightened that she uses any means she can to hold on to people. There's a lot of seduction, but I see it more as a pregenital seduction, a desire to merge with mother or with a maternal father. She doesn't sound ready for an adult relationship."

"Meaning I shouldn't marry her."

"Meaning, from what I'm hearing, I think that would be a mistake."

"Then what do you recommend? Should I just keep working with her as best I can?"

"Do you think you can?"

"I don't know." I shook my head. "I really don't know."

"I'd recommend you refer her to another therapist. Perhaps a woman. That's what I'd recommend."

I left his office still in a muddle. As soon as I returned to my own office I went to my bookshelf to find the book by Balint that my supervisor had recommended. I sat in my office the rest of the evening reading the passage about "malignant regression." The description *did* seem to fit Jennifer's case. Balint wrote, "As long as the patient's expectations and demands are met, the therapist is allowed to observe most interesting, revealing events and *pari passu* his patient will feel better, appreciative and grateful." But this was only one side of the coin, Balint warned. If the patient's expectations were not met, the patient would plunge into "unending suffering" or "unending vituperation" or both. Once that situation had established itself the analyst would find it more and more difficult to control the therapy, and still more difficult to terminate the relationship. He cited Breuer's treatment of Anna O. and Ferenczi's use of mutual analysis, noting that in these cases there had been a kind of vicious spiral in which, no sooner had some of a patient's "cravings" been satisfied, new cravings appeared, demanding to be almost immediately satisfied, leading eventually to a development of what Balint called "addiction-like states." He observed that such malignant regressions, when they went unchecked, often led to a "tragic or heroic finale."

Balint was not sure precisely where this addiction to regression might come from, but speculated that it went back to infancy. He alluded to psychoanalytic literature about the passionate nature of childhood wishes, fantasies and instinctual behavior, and about children who were subjected to unusually traumatic experiences. He also speculated that such traumatic experiences led to cravings, needs, passionate desires and a "great proneness to sexual seduction" and "acting-out types of hysterical states." He said that in the therapy relationship such patients have an unconscious aim of using the regression to gain gratification through "external action"—inducing the therapist to act out. They usually suffer from a "fairly severe form of hysteria," and derive a "fair amount of secondary gain from their illness," generally by using it to obtain sympathy and action from the therapist. Also, according to Balint, they strive to form a mutually trusting relationship with the therapist that replicates the symbiotic relationship they once had with their mother. However, "since the mutually trusting relationship is highly precariously balanced, the . . . unsuspecting atmosphere breaks down repeatedly, and frequently symptoms of desperate clinging develop as safeguards and reassurance against another possible breakdown."

I put Balint's book aside and picked up Ferenczi's collected papers. Ferenczi had been the first psychoanalayst to allude to the treatment of multiple personalities and to connect them with childhood traumas. In his paper "Confusion of Tongues between Adults and the Child," in which he spoke about the sexual abuse by parents at a time when even the psychoanalytic establishment was not able to hear it, he wrote in 1932: "If the traumatic events accumulate during the life of the growing person, the number and variety of personality splits increase, and soon it will be rather difficult to maintain contact without confusion with all the fragments, which all act as separate personalities but mostly do not know each other." In working with such patients, Ferenczi deviated from Freud's standard method, practicing a form of mutual analysis in which he allowed patients to analyze him as he analyzed them. He also had patients sit on his lap and pretend he was their father, and would often see them in four- or five-hour sessions in order to help them regress to their infantile points of fixation and release them cathartically. One patient in particular, Elizabeth Severn, a beautiful dancer who entered a training analysis with Ferenczi, seems to have captured his heart. She was mentioned by him in several of his papers, and he also referred to her in his notes. She later became an analyst herself and wrote a rather mystical book, taking credit for Ferenczi's technique of mutual analysis. Unfortunately, rumors gradually spread that Ferenczi was getting too involved with Severn and other patients and he was ostracized by the psychoanalytic community. He died suddenly at the age of sixty.

Balint noted that after Ferenczi's death the psychoanalytic community became factionalized over the question of the use of regression and catharsis in therapy. One faction saw regression as necessary and useful (Balint was in that camp, as well as Lowen, the founder of bioenergetics), while the other faction saw it as a dangerous by-product of analysis that had to be carefully controlled.

I thought about the fate of Ferenczi for a while, sitting by the window of my office, staring out at the park. Had I, like Ferenczi, gone too far? By encouraging Jennifer's regression, had I played with fire? I got up to retrieve my copy of Breuer's case history about Anna O and reread it. I noted how dependent Anna O.—who had a dual personality—had become on Breuer. In fact, when another doctor tried to examine her, she refused even to acknowledge his presence in the room. And when this new doctor blew smoke in her face to get her to look at him, she "rushed to the door to take away the key and fell unconscious to the ground." Breuer and only Breuer could get her to eat when she had not eaten for days, to speak when she had not spoken for days, and to sleep when she had not slept for days. Whenever he had to skip a session or two (he saw her twice a day, seven days a week) to go on a trip, she invariably grew worse. She became hysterically attached to Breuer, so that in the end he had to get away from her, off on a second honeymoon with his wife.

After rereading this case I turned to the one about Jung, to which my supervisor had referred. While working as a staff psychiatrist at the Burghölzli Mental Hospital, Jung treated a beautiful young woman of eighteen named Sabina Spielrein who was suffering from schizophrenia. After "curing" her, he fell in love with her and they had an affair. When she later complained to Freud about it, Freud chastised Jung. In a long, rambling letter to Freud, Jung repented: "I . . . deplore the sins I have committed, for I am largely to blame for the high-flying hopes of my former patient. . . . I imputed all the other wishes and hopes [to have an affair] entirely to my patient without seeing the same thing in myself. . . . In view of the fact that the patient had shortly before been my friend and enjoyed my full confidence, my action was a piece of knavery which I very reluctantly confess to you as my father."

Was Jennifer like Anna O.? Elizabeth Severn? Sabina Spielrein? Was I like Breuer, Ferenczi or Jung? Apparently my supervisor thought so. I thought about what Balint had written and tried to relate it to my work with Jennifer. I could see how Jennifer had let me see "most interesting and revealing events" (her transformations into different personalities), while at the same time making sure I was aware that I was the first to be honored with these secrets. Indeed, I had long felt her hypnotic pull, and understood that multiples were *innately* familiar with hypnosis, making unconscious use of it themselves in changing personalities. I was familiar with the research by Kluft and others that affirmed that multiples were the best subjects for hypnosis and were generally "psychic." I also knew about David Caul's famous statement that multiples could "smell a liar at a thousand paces in one ten-thousandth of a second."

Jennifer also seemed to fit Balint's description in other ways. She appeared to be on a spiral of never-ending expectations, which Balint noted was common in the cases of both male and female patients he studied, and there was the threat of severely destructive acting out if I did not live up to them: "Please, please be my Good Daddy, not my Bad Daddy! Don't leave me or I'll kill myself," she seemed to be saying. There was an immediate, extreme dependence on me and a demand for my complete loyalty and unconditional love that seemed to relate to her early infantile relationship with her mother. And, of course, there was her courtship of me—with flowers, letters, poems and the like—which seemed to be what Balint meant when he wrote about the "proneness to sexual seduction." And, yes, she did seem to use her illness to gain sympathy.

In view of what I had read, it seemed that I really had no other choice but to refer her to someone else, as my supervisor recommended.

Maybe he's wrong, I said to myself. Maybe he didn't understand things as much as he thought. Maybe I hadn't explained it to him well enough. He really didn't know the kind of person Jennifer was.

There were many sleepless nights, and many headaches, but by the time I saw Jennifer for her regular session on the afternoon of September 26, I had made up my mind.

"JENNIFER, THERE'S something I want to tell you."

She sat on the couch, her body still, her face drawn, not looking at me. She had come a few minutes late, as though in anticipation of what I was going to say. "I think I know what it is," she said. "You can't see me anymore, right?"

"That's sort of it." I felt a bubble of sadness in my throat but tried not to show it. "I can't see you anymore as a therapist. We can still be friends."

"Why?"

"Because I can't handle being your therapist. I'm not skilled enough to be your therapist, not together enough myself."

"I'll never find another therapist as good as you," she said, a tear in her eye. I smiled and nodded. "I think you're skilled enough."

"I'm overinvolved. Drained. I've lost my objectivity. And that's no good."

"I see. . . ."

"I'm not abandoning you. Not deserting you. I really would like to be friends with you at some point. But I think it would be best if I referred you to another therapist. I was thinking maybe this time you ought to try a female. I know some good ones. As I've said before, I think you're ready now for analysis."

"Why do you think I need a female analyst?"

"You've seen five male analysts now, and none has worked out entirely. You've played out a pattern with your male analysts, a pattern related to your father. The end of the pattern is that they leave you. You need to understand that pattern. That's what analysis would do, help you understand that and other patterns. You might have the same or similar pattern with a female therapist. But a female might not be as susceptible to you."

She did a double take when I said that, and a rueful smirk crept into the corners of her mouth. I felt immediately sorry I had said it. "I'm not sure what you're saying. Are you saying you're too susceptible to me and that's why you can't see me any longer?"

"That's one way of looking at it."

"So you're saying it's my fault."

"In analysis we don't look for faults, we look for reasons."

"Well, however you say it, it seems as if you're blaming me for something, as if you're not taking responsibility for your part."

"I said I thought I wasn't together enough."

"That's true."

She gazed at me thoughtfully for a moment, then looked down. I waited, letting what I had said settle in. I had dreaded this session for several days and now I had another headache. I felt impatient to get the session over with, to be out of it. I looked forward to being friends with her, if that was possible. But I did not want to be responsible for her any longer. It was too heavy a burden.

She shook her head, gazing at the floor. She had expected this, but it had still stunned her. She would tell me later that all her personalities were speaking inside her head at once. Mildred was saying to keep calm. Margaret was talking about going to a lawyer. Tom was saying "I told you so." Mary was assuring everyone that everything would be all right. She looked up at last and said, "Maybe you're right. Maybe it would be best for me to see a woman. You're right, I really haven't had a very good experience with male therapists. Or with men in general."

"No, you haven't." I was relieved that she seemed to be taking it calmly. "How do you feel about me now?"

"I'm not sure. Mixed."

"What's the mix?"

"I suppose I feel a little hurt. And sad. I'll miss you."

"You may have more feelings about this by the next session. We'll continue on until you find someone else. I'll give you a few referrals so you can pick the person you like best."

"That's very kind of you."

"You sound sarcastic."

"Do I? I didn't mean to." She sighed. "I suppose it *is* a bit of a shock."

"I understand."

"You said that we could be friends 'at some point.' I'm just wondering what you meant by that?"

"I just think we both need a period of separateness."

"I see. How long would we have to be separate?"

"I'm not sure."

"When will you know?"

"Maybe by next week's session."

We then spoke coolly about the termination process and about the "prospect of being friends." At the end of the session she got up, smiling very brightly, and said, "See you Wednesday."

"See you then."

After she left, I thought: I hope she doesn't have a relapse. God, I hope she doesn't have a relapse. I went to the small refrigerator in the kitchen near the waiting area and put some water on for tea. I sat in the chair by the window, looking out, feeling the bubble in my throat again, suddenly overwhelmed with deep sadness. The teapot began to whistle but I sat in my chair without moving. I sat there while all the water boiled out.

I KEPT vacillating, one moment feeling fine about the decision to refer Jennifer to another therapist, the next thinking it was all wrong and feeling resentful and jealous of the notion of another therapist taking over after I had made such progress with her. Then I would wonder if I had really made progress, or whether all of it was illusory, whether she was just pretending to get better in order to win my love and approval.

To strengthen my resolve I reread Freud's paper on transference-love. Freud unequivocally advised against a therapist having a real relationship with a patient. Referring to the common experience of a young woman falling in love with her male therapist, he stated flatly that if the patient makes advances and the therapist returns them, "She would have succeeded in what all patients struggle for, in expressing in action, in reproducing in real life, what she ought only to remember, to reproduce as the content of her mind and to retain within the mental sphere." Freud added that when this happened, "all the inhibitions and pathological reactions" of the patient's neurosis would surface, with no possibility for the analyst to correct them, so that "the painful episode would end in remorse." Noting that younger men were especially tempted by such patients, he wrote that rejecting a young woman's plea for romance was a difficult thing for them to do, pointing out that there was "an incomparable fascination about a noble woman who confesses her passion." He warned that every psychoanalyst had a threefold battle to wage: the battle against the forces in his own mind that would draw him "below the level of analysis"; the forces from the outside world that were always critical of psychoanalysis and its attempt to reveal the dark underside of human behavior; and the forces of patients who at first scoff at psychoanalysis but then disclose the "overestimation of sexual life" that holds them captive and drives them to induce the therapist to join them in acting out. He concluded: "The psychoanalyst knows that the forces he works with are of the most explosive kind and that he needs as much caution and conscientiousness as a chemist."

No matter how many times I read this paper, I could not at that time become convinced by it (although now I have come to accept it entirely). I could not help but think that my relationship with Jennifer was an exception. I could not accept that it was just transference and countertransference. Freud did not seem to think that it was possible for a genuine, healthy relationship to develop between a patient and doctor. According to him, healthy relationships between men and women could only occur between mature individuals—those who had successfully traversed the various critical stages of early childhood without suffering major psychic traumas and becoming blocked, "genital characters" relating to and forming lasting attachments with other people not as narcissistic extensions of themselves but as separate individuals. Was Jennifer such an individual? Was I? Were there *any* mature people left on the planet? Or was maturity just an idealistic concept to be strived for, never to be entirely achieved?

In the middle of such heavy questions I received a phone call from Jennifer. "I'm afraid of falling apart," she said.

"You'd better come in."

SHE WAS sitting on the edge of the couch with that old look of desperation, the look she'd had in the beginning. Once again she was rocking back and forth. "After our last session I felt really depressed," she told me. "I kept thinking . . . about cutting myself."

"Do you think you're going to do it?"

"I don't know."

"Did you contact any of the other analysts yet?"

"No."

"Jennifer, you've got to call another analyst," I said, raising my voice a notch. Actually I was doing quite a job of containing the anger I felt at that moment, anger I knew was out of proportion to the situation and which I did not fully understand. She had suddenly become to me like some spider crawling up my back, one I could not get rid of. It was like she had stung me, and the anger I now felt was her anger, which she had injected into me. "I can't be your therapist anymore, I just can't. I'm sorry." I looked at her with stern, distant eyes. "Where's the list of analysts I gave you? In your purse?"

"I left it at home. Why?"

"I wanted to go over them with you. It might help you decide if I give you more information about each of them. It doesn't matter. I remember their names."

"I don't want to go over them."

"Why not?"

"I don't know." She hated hearing me talk to her in that tone of voice she would later tell me. That was just how her other therapists had eventually talked to her. Sooner or later they all used that tone with her. She had thought it would be different this time. She never thought I would turn out the same as the others. It seemed to her that we had established some kind of deep bond through the work we had done together and the secrets she had shared and I had witnessed. This tone of voice coming from a man she had come to idealize and depend on with her very being was like hot lava burning down the insides of her body. She could have exploded at any minute.

"Jennifer," I went on, tiredly, impatiently, "I just can't do it anymore."

"I understand."

"I'm burned out."

"Right." Her face tightened and a whimper came from her.

"Would you please call the phone numbers I gave you?"

"Yes." She sat hunched over, her eyes downcast. I could see she had no intention of calling them.

"What is it?" I asked in a softer voice.

"Nothing."

"Doesn't look like nothing to me."

She broke into tears and cried softly, hugging herself. "It hurts . . . to be . . . dismissed. . . ." I let her cry for a while. Then she stopped and gazed silently at the floor, her eyes downward so that I could see only the tops of her pupils, dark blue now and focused nowhere in the shadow of the room. She looked so very sad, but somehow gracefully sad, with one leg curled around another and her head cocked a bit to one side. Then, somehow, she came out of it. Her eyes lifted and she turned her gaze to me and actually smiled.

"I guess it'll just take some getting used to," she said.

I nodded, touched, ready to call the whole thing off. Instead, I said, "Are you going to be okay?"

"Yes." She smiled. "I'll be okay."

"ALL WEEKEND I felt torn apart," she told me. "At one moment Margaret would go to the phone to dial your number, all set to tell you off. Then Mildred would take over and put the phone down and suggest that everybody keep their heads and be *logical* about it. Then Jenny would take over and roll up in a ball on the rug sucking her thumb. Then Tom would take out the knife you gave him and go to the window to throw it out. But before he could get there Mary would come out and put the knife away. Several times I went into the bathroom and took out a razor blade. I'd sit on the toilet seat holding the razor in my hand, trying to work up the guts to do it. Then Margaret or Mildred would take over, toss the razor away and do the dishes or vacuum the floor for the third time."

Somehow she had managed to make it through the weekend and now she sat in front of me with a pouty face, disheveled hair and bloodshot eyes. I felt no sympathy for her.

"Are you still feeling suicidal?" I asked as calmly as I could.

"Yes . . . a little. . . ." She looked up anxiously.

I was tapping my fingers nervously on the arm of the chair. "You're trying emotional blackmail," I told her, leaning toward her ever so calmly—but my fingers were still tapping. "You were conditioned by your upbringing to use sickness and helplessness to get people to care about you. Now you're doing that with me. You're saying, Stay with me or I'll fall apart. Don't leave me or I'll commit suicide—"

"I'm *not* trying to blackmail you. I can't help it if I'm feeling this way."

"All right, all right." I had to restrain myself from shaking her. I felt desperate, in a rage . . . I would never be able to get rid of her, she would embed herself in my office like some bat in the belfry, and suck my blood forever. "Never mind. Have you phoned any of the analysts yet?"

"No, I haven't."

"When are you going to?"

"I don't know."

"Jennifer, I can't handle you anymore," I said, standing up, pacing about the room. My voice exploded out of me. "Try to understand. I can't *do it*. I can't . . ." I was about ready to get down on my knees and beg her.

"What about me? What about what *I* need?"

"I can't deal with your needs right now."

"So I see."

I sat down again and looked past her out the window. We sat for what seemed a long time in silence. We could hear children in the park shrieking about some kind of game.

"Jennifer?" My voice was near-pleading now. "Jennifer, will you please phone them?"

"*Yes.*" It came out like a hiss. "Yes, I'll call them. *Okay?* I'll call them tomorrow. . . ."

That was to be our last session.

A TELEPHONE CALL

I SAT in my apartment at the end of a long day in which I had seen twelve patients. It had been a month since I had last seen Jennifer. I picked up the phone and dialed her number.

"Jennifer? It's Gerry."

"Oh." She didn't sound exactly pleased to hear from me.

"I'm calling to see how you are."

"I'm fine."

"Good." A pause. "How's your analysis going?"

"Just fine, thank you."

"Well, how's everything else? Have you begun dancing again?"

"I started classes a week ago."

"That's good."

"Yes, it *is* good."

"I'm glad for you."

"Thanks. I don't mean to be rude but I have to go. I was just on my way out the door when you called."

"I understand. I was wondering . . . I was wondering if you'd like to have lunch sometime?"

"Actually, no. I have to run. I'm on my way to a dance class."

"You'd better run, then."

A pause.

"Take care," she said.

"You too."

"Goodbye."

"Goodbye, then."

AN INTERLUDE

AND SO the therapy with Jennifer had come to an abrupt end. It had lasted only slightly longer than one summer, beginning in the green months of April, ending in the yellow sun of August. But within that short time more had happened to me, of an emotional, involving nature, than had happened since my childhood. The experience had left me in a state of nervous exhaustion and confusion that took me several months to recover from.

As I look back on it now, it remains the most intense and vivid therapy experience of my career, in a way, I think, comparable to one's first adolescent love affair. In spite of all the transference-countertransference problems that derailed the therapy, it was still an amazing treatment. All at once her personalities had begun to capitulate like dominoes, under the sway of our unusually intimate working alliance. All at once she was aware of everything and the repressed memories and feelings were gushing out. I have worked with other multiples since then, and with other severely disturbed patients, but never has so much progress been made in such a short time. Nor, in fact, have I read of another case like it in the literature. In a sense, it was the best of times because both of us were extremely motivated to give ourselves to the therapy, she out of a desperate need to shrug off her tortured existence and I out of a similarly desperate need to throw myself into an experience, to forget certain things, to prove certain things. But it was also the worst of times because I was giving myself over to the therapeutic task for the wrong reasons and with a false confidence, which had brought it to an end prematurely.

During the winter months I took many walks around Manhattan. I had never looked at Manhattan so closely or been so fascinated with the buildings, the gardens, the people. I would leave my apartment on a Saturday morning, not knowing where I was going. I would walk all day, always to a section I had never explored before. Each day I would discover a new garden or mall, an odd building, a mysterious corridor between buildings, or a new neighborhood. Once I discovered an alley between high-rise buildings. It was blocked by a latticed iron doorway but the door was open, so I went down the alley to explore. At the end of the alley was an open courtyard pocketed in the center of a block of buildings. In the middle of the courtyard was a little white cabin that was being used as a law office. The cabin looked very old. I felt as though I had just discovered an ancient treasure in the middle of Manhattan.

For several months I took these walks, thinking of nothing in particular, no matter how cold or whether there was snow or sleet on the ground. In fact, I took pleasure in trudging through the snow and became fascinated with the various shapes of the icicles hanging from trees and buildings, fancying that I was becoming an expert on icicle shapes. I even went back to the cabin between buildings to check on the state of the icicles there.

Meanwhile, I would read about Jennifer in the entertainment pages, how she had started a small company of her own, how she was making a comeback, how she was creating new dances, and I would see advertisements about her appearances at various theatres around town.

Winter faded to spring, then summer, and in the hot days of shimmering cement and melted tar on asphalt street I lost my desire to walk. I began to lose interest in the city, and at the same time to think again about Jennifer. I realized I missed her. I wanted to see her.

A NIGHT AT THE BALLET

A YEAR later. Jennifer was on the stage of the Joyce Theatre performing in a ballet she had also choreographed. I was in the audience, a proud smile on my face.

She had taken a piece of music that many had tried unsuccessfully to choreograph—Stravinsky's *L'Histoire du soldat*—and had come up with what, I felt, would surely become the definitive ballet. The comic invention of her choreography was equal to the brilliant comedic strains of the music, and her dancing—as the charming princess—was also inventive and enchanting. However, the *pièce de résistance* of the ballet occurred in between sections of the score, when she came downstage and sang the chorale in a sweet, vibrant, childlike voice, accompanied only by a flute and bass violin, rousing the audience to applaud for several minutes. The ballet truly displayed her versatility.

The curtain fell to a standing ovation, and Jennifer received eleven curtain calls. I felt like a proud mother or father experiencing each expression of gratitude and joy on her face as if it signaled my own.

Afterward I ambled somewhat anxiously to the stage entrance, holding a tulip in my hand. I told the guard I wanted to see Jennifer, half-hoping to be turned away, not quite sure how she would receive me or how I would react to her. He let me in and I squeezed down a long, narrow hallway to a row of dressing rooms full of chattering dancers. I stopped at one with Jennifer's name on it. I knocked on the door and a gray-haired woman came out.

"Is Jennifer there?"

"Who's asking?"

"Tell her it's . . . Gerry."

"Just a minute."

She disappeared, then a moment later, there she was, still in her costume—a long, purple, diaphanous gown—smiling with delight. She did not seem in the least surprised to see me; rather, she seemed to have expected me, as though in her intuitive way she had always known that our two journeys would merge on this very night.

"Gerry," she said matter-of-factly. "How nice of you." She took a step toward me and extended her arms for an embrace. I accepted it awkwardly, my arms hanging at my sides, still trying to make the transition from therapist to friend.

"I just wanted to stop by and tell you how much I enjoyed your performance—and your choreography," I said in a voice that was trying hard to remain calm. "And to give you this." I presented her with the tulip, bowing in exaggerated fashion.

"Oh, thank you." She curtsied, took the flower, sniffed it and held it against her breasts with both hands. "I'm really glad you could come."

"I wouldn't have missed it. Really, it was terrific."

"Thanks."

"I know you must be tired so I won't keep you."

"Would you like to come in for a minute?" She nodded toward her dressing room.

"Sure."

"It's a little messy. And claustrophobic."

"I'll try to adjust."

She led me into the dressing room, which was thick with the aroma of greasepaint, and shut the door behind us, leaving the gray-haired woman outside. The room had pink velvet wallpaper and was about the size of a large walk-in closet. At one end was a costume rack bearing an array of gowns, belts, tutus, hats, scarves, tights, leotards, shoes; at the other end was a dressing table with a large mirror, the edges of which had been decked with telegrams from well-wishers. There were two wooden chairs with red velvet cushions.

"Have a seat," she said, whirling to put the flower into a large vase that already contained several dozen others. She moved gracefully about the room as though still in her ballet role, and when she sat down, she straddled the chair. There was a pause as we eyed one another with awkward smiles. "Well," she said, "would you like a glass of champagne?" She picked up a half-empty bottle from the dressing table. "It may be a little flat by now, but it's a good brand." She raised and lowered her brows, grinning.

"No, thanks. I'll pass."

"So, how are you anyway?"

"Pretty good."

"And your practice?"

"Very good, thanks."

"Glad to hear it."

"I'd ask how you are but obviously you're doing fine. You've gotten right back into the swing of things. And you look really great."

"I feel great."

"You look it."

She did look striking, more striking than ever before. It was not simply her beautiful gown or the stage makeup, which accented her brows, eyes and lips. Rather, it came from her expressions, her movements, her posture, all of which conveyed a new confidence, a new sense of worth, and most of all a new aura of inner calm. To be sure, a dance triumph such as the one she had experienced would make anybody feel better about herself; on the other hand, in order to score such a triumph one would have to feel pretty good in the first place.

I smiled at her with a mix of pride and joy—and she sat back beaming.

"I was really impressed with your choreography," I said, becoming less stiff and more animated. "It's special to see a dance that's both funny and sad all at the same time. I was thinking that several parts of you must have had a hand in creating it."

"Actually, I don't think of myself in terms of parts anymore," she replied rather quickly.

"Oh? Good. Then you're completely integrated?"

"I wouldn't say *completely*."

"You still have separate thoughts and feelings about things?"

"Not exactly." She smiled at me the way one might smile at a child. "Gerry, you're not my shrink anymore."

"You're *right*." I laughed. What else could I do?

"You were a wonderful shrink, and I've come to really appreciate what you did, but you can't be my shrink anymore."

"I agree, absolutely."

"We're not going to quarrel, are we? On our first meeting as ordinary citizens?"

"Definitely not."

"Or maybe we should." She smiled mischievously. "Maybe it would do us some good."

"Oh?"

"Then we could stop being so terribly nice and good-humored."

We looked at one another for a long moment, smiling at first, then not smiling, our eyes taking each other in almost as though we had never seen each other before. Indeed, we had *not* seen each other before in this way.

"I was just thinking," she said, "there's a quaint little coffee shop on the corner on Sixth Avenue."

"Which corner?"

"The northwest corner of Fifty-sixth Street."

"Yes, I know the place."

"It has yellow awnings."

"With pictures of clowns on them."

"And inside there's an autographed photo of Charlie Chaplin holding his cane over his head."

"And another of Marilyn Monroe's white dress blowing up into the air."

"You *do* know the place."

"I've been there many times. It's one of my favorites."

"Do you think we can be friends, Gerry? Do you think enough time has passed?"

"I think so. . . ."

"But is it . . . proper?"

"You mean for a therapist and former patient to be friends? Why not? Freud did it. He was friends with Marie Bonaparte."

"She was a special person, though. A princess, wasn't she?"

"He was friends with paupers too. The Wolf Man was a pauper at the end. He lost all his money during the Bolshevik Revolution. Anyway, you're a special person, too."

"Thanks. Yes, I think I *am* special, actually." She jutted out her lower lip in a proud smile. "I'll accept that compliment. I can accept compliments now. See how mature I am?" We both laughed and she studied me for a moment. "You know, I was just thinking that in a way you seem like a stranger."

"I guess in a way I am. I was always hiding behind the blank screen before."

"So now I have something to look forward to. Getting to know the real you."

"I suppose you do. And I can get to know the new you."

"Yes, yes."

She jumped up in a perky, dancelike move. "I'll just be a minute. I have to change into my street clothes. Unless you want me to go with you in this?" She whirled about, smiling, holding out her skirt.

"That would be okay."

"It's nice to see you again, Gerry."

"It's great to see you again."

She rushed up to me, came to a sudden stop and planted a kiss on my forehead.

"I won't be long."

"Take your time."

"I'll just slip on a pair of jeans. Jeans will be fine for that coffee shop, right?"

"I'd say so."

"Gerry, could I ask a favor? Unfortunately I don't have a screen to dress behind. This dressing room's too small for a screen. Would you mind terribly waiting outside while I change?"

"No, of course not." I got up.

"Thanks."

"You're welcome," I said, going to the door. "It's the least I could do for a friend."

POSTSCRIPT

JENNIFER EVENTUALLY retired from dance and became a successful businesswoman. Recently she enrolled in a Ph.D. program. She no longer sees a therapist, and she still has her separate personalities, nearly a decade later. However, for the most part her personalities remain conscious of one another, and she has had no relapses. She has been married for several years and lives in the East.

I have gone on to write several books on psychoanalytic theory and psychotherapy. Through additional supervision, training and experience, I think I have learned to master my countertransference and to become at least a competent therapist.

The author has quoted briefly from the following works:

Michael Balint, *The Basic Fault: Therapeutic Aspects of Regression.* London: Tavistock, 1968.

Josef Breuer and Sigmund Freud, *Studies on Hysteria.* Translated by James Strachey. New York: Basic Books, 1957.

Linda Donn, *Freud and Jung: Years of Friendship, Years of Loss.* New York: Charles Scribner's Sons, 1988.

Sandor Ferenczi, "Confusion of Tongues between Adults and the Child." *Final Contributions to the Problems and Methods of Psycho-Analysis,* Translated by Eric Mosbacher. New York: Brunner/Mazel, 1980.

Sigmund Freud, "Observations on Transference-Love." *Collected Papers. Vol. 2,* Translated by Joan Riviere. New York: Basic Books, 1959.

Sigmund Freud, "Recommendations for Physicians on the Psycho-analytic Method of Treatment." *Collected Papers. Vol. 2,* Translated by Joan Riviere. New York: Basic Books, 1959.

Ernest Freud, ed. *The Letters of Sigmund Freud.* New York: Basic Books, 1960.